C000176618

Somerset

40 Town and Country Walks

The authors and publisher have made every effort to ensure that the information in this publication is accurate, and accept no responsibility whatsoever for any loss, injury or inconvenience experienced by any person or persons whilst using this book.

published by
pocket mountains ltd
The Old Church, Annanside,
Moffat DG10 9HB

ISBN: 978-1-907025-68-6

Text and photography copyright © John and Annie Fergusson 2018

The right of John and Annie Fergusson to be identified as the Authors of this work has been asserted by them in accordance with the Copyright, Designs and Patents Act 1988

A catalogue record for this book is available from the British Library

Contains Ordnance Survey data © Crown copyright and database right 2018 supported by out of copyright mapping 1945-1961

All rights reserved. No part of this publication may be reproduced, stored in a retrieval system, or transmitted in any form or by any means, electronic or mechanical, including photocopying and recording, unless expressly permitted by Pocket Mountains Ltd.

Printed in Poland

Introduction

Ah, Somerset! Even the name brings on a warm glow, conjuring up images of apple orchards, thatched cottages and wildflower meadows. Somerset is all of those and more. It's the home of cider and the Glastonbury Festival. It is the place where King Alfred burned cakes and defeated Danes, and where, some say, King Arthur held court at Camelot. It is a land of history and heroes, of moorland and marsh, heritage railways and hi-tech helicopters, of beauty and mystery in equal measure. What other county in England can boast such a variety of scenery as Somerset? And there can surely be none with such extremes of topography. At one end (literally) is the great upland wilderness of Exmoor, at the other the pastoral tranquility of the apple orchards.

The geological violence of the Cheddar and Ebbor Gorges is but a stone's throw from the wetlands of the Avalon Marshes. Climb to any summit in the Mendip or Quantock Hills, or a mound like Burrow Mump, and the view extends over billiard-table-smooth flatlands to the next hill or range beyond. It is an extraordinary landscape with no fewer than five ranges of hills, a National Park, dramatic coastline and one of the most extensive flatland expanses in the country. Who could fail to be charmed by villages with names like Stogumber, Westonzoyland, Mudgely or Hornblotton? And when the names are double-barrelled, they sound like members of a pre-war varsity cricket team: Nempnett Thrubwell, Haselbury Plucknett, Peasedown St John, Norton Malreward, Sutton Montis, Shepton Mallet and Huish Champflower (with Rodney Stoke to drive the bus). There are endless places to go and an extensive network of paths and byways to help you get there. Whether you are a casual walker out for a stroll or an experienced hiker planning a day in the hills, Somerset has something to suit. The locals are friendly and the facilities are excellent. What's more, you're never too far from a refreshing glass of cider or cream tea when you need one. Somerset in a nutshell? Warm, welcoming and waiting to be explored!

History

Britain's oldest complete human skeleton was discovered at the turn of the 20th century in a cavern in Cheddar Gorge. Cheddar Man, as he's become known, lived at the end of the last ice age and DNA testing has revealed that his direct descendants are still living in the area some 9000 years later.

In Cheddar Man's day, much of Somerset was disappearing under rising sea levels, creating a vast expanse of shallow saltwater. Slowly it turned into saltmarshes, then became cut off from the sea. Four thousand years after the death of Cheddar Man, it had been transformed into a great freshwater lagoon, its pools and channels rich in fish, fowl and wildlife.

Neolithic man built wooden walkways to travel between patches of dry land – examples have been found which date from around 3000BC, the woodwork largely preserved by the peat into which it eventually sank.

Early man has left his mark all across Somerset, in hillforts like Dolebury, Ham Hill and Cadbury. Ancient earthworks are scattered over the county: barrows, mounds, and stone circles. Evidence of Roman occupation can be seen in the magnificent remains in Bath and in the Roman roads which have survived, notably the Fosse Way. The Romans extracted salt from the levels and mined lead from the Mendips. It was several centuries after the Romans' departure, incidentally, that the first documented use of 'Somerset' occurred: the 9th-century Anglo-Saxon Chronicle recorded the *Sumorsaete* as a people living in the area in 845AD. That century, the marshes came to the rescue of Alfred the Great by providing a safe haven from the Danes until he was strong enough to defeat Guthrum's army at The Battle of Ethandun.

In the centuries that followed, Somerset was no stranger to warfare. In 1642, the first shots of the English Civil War were fired in Somerset, when Royalists ambushed a contingent of Parliamentarians near Street. The last battle ever fought on English soil took place at Sedgemoor in July 1685, when the Duke of Monmouth's rebel 'army' was defeated. His supporters were then rounded up and summarily tried in Taunton by Judge Jeffreys. In what has become known as 'The Bloody Assizes', the guilty were sentenced to death or transportation.

The Industrial Revolution, which so changed the Midlands and northern counties of England, had less physical effect on the South West, although its impact was far reaching. Cottage industries withered away with few sizeable factories to replace them. The wool trade, so important to Exmoor in particular, moved nearer to the mills in the north. Leadmines in the Mendips were exhausted and it had become too costly to take iron ore from the Brendon Hills. Coalfields in the north of the county were hard to reach and the costly canal built to service them was soon killed off by the railway (which was in turn closed in the 1960s' Beeching cuts). Somerset today is not without its industry but essentially it remains the rural, agricultural economy it has always been, although today tourism also plays a major part.

Walking in Somerset

There is no better way to enjoy the Somerset countryside than by walking through it. With thousands of miles of public footpaths, an endless variety of quiet country roads and an increasing amount of 'open access' land, there is plenty of scope to devise the perfect walk.

Somerset is criss-crossed by long-distance routes like the South West Coast Path, the Coleridge Way and the River Parrett Trail. On the whole, footpaths are well marked from public roads, although many signposts are broken or concealed in the undergrowth. Waymarkers are commonplace and the colours used on the arrows or posts denote how they may be used: footpaths, shown in yellow, are restricted to walkers; blue indicates bridleways, which are open to cyclists, horse riders and walkers, and red marks a byway which can also be used by motor vehicles. Good boots are advisable for all routes and essential for some, particularly the Cheddar Gorge walk where the paths are both rocky and steep. It is important to keep to the established routes and not to stray onto private land, although if the right of way lies across a field of crops and is unclear, it is better to walk around the edge of the field until you can rejoin the path. Some stiles are showing their age and, while they are gradually being replaced by gates, you will almost certainly have to cross stiles during your time in Somerset. Check each for its structural integrity and slipperiness before putting your trust in it.

Nettles and brambles can make walking in shorts a painful experience so it is sensible to wear long trousers when venturing into the Somerset countryside. Avoid climbing over walls, leave gates as you find them, and, of course, take your litter home. If you are walking with a dog, keep it under close control, avoid livestock and make sure you clean up after it. Finally, always make sure that someone knows where you are planning to walk and when you expect to get home.

Beware of ticks

Ticks are a national problem, but Exmoor is a hotspot. Ticks lurk in long grass, bracken and woodland; their bites are painless but can cause Lyme Disease which, if left untreated, can have very serious consequences. Sensible precautions include keeping your skin covered, tucking your trouser bottoms into socks, and wearing shoes or boots rather than sandals. It is a good idea to use insect repellent on clothing and exposed skin. Check yourself and your companions – human or canine – for ticks at the end of the walk. Remove any attached ticks with a removal tool designed for the purpose (available in all outdoors shops) as soon as you can. Don't let the thought of them put you off your walk, but do be aware and take precautions.

Wildlife and nature

You only have to count the number of nature conservation designations in Somerset to realise how special it is; there are 127 Sites of Special Scientific Interest (SSSIs), 70 Nature Reserves, 15 National Nature Reserves, 11 Special Areas of

Conservation, four Areas of Outstanding Natural Beauty (AONB), two Special Protection Areas and a National Park. Collectively they cover a host of different habitats, from coastal saltmarsh to floodplain grazing marshland, from upland heath to lowland meadows and almost all of it is under some form of threat. A combination of climate change, farming practices, unsympathetic development and pollution has caused the recent disappearance of several species, such as grass-of-Parnassus, pearl-bordered fritillary butterfly and red grouse.

Somerset is home to seven species which are threatened with global extinction and more than 200 'priority species' on the UK Biodiversity Action Plan, such as the water vole and hairy click beetle. Britain's largest wild animals, red deer, which have roamed Exmoor since prehistoric times, are also feeling the pressure. They're being hunted by poachers cashing in on the increasing demand for venison. Exmoor ponies, on the other hand, have made a comeback since the post-World War II years when there were fears for the breed's survival. Determined and careful management has seen numbers increase and the future now seems more secure.

Other successes include the large blue butterfly which died out in Britain in the 1970s and has been successfully reintroduced. Common crane, missing from England's wetlands for centuries, are back, and the decline of the bittern, once down to just a handful of males, appears to have been reversed. The organisations which look after the Somerset countryside and habitats, many relying on volunteers, are doing a marvellous job. Information boards, which can be found at many sites and reserves, are well worth studying and local tourist information offices and Exmoor National Park centres have leaflets and displays to help you get the most from your visit.

Getting around

Somerset is one of England's larger counties, yet it has one of the lowest population densities and bus services are thin on the ground as a result. Where applicable, this guide provides information about the nearest bus stops to allow you to join the walk. Bus services do change and it is advisable to check routes and timetables before setting out. Similarly, where train stations are convenient, they are mentioned in the notes preceding the walk. For car drivers, this guide will direct you towards free parking where it is available and, where it is not, to a car park where a modest charge may be required. Some car parks have height restricting barriers. If you park at the roadside, do not block access and keep clear of passing places.

Using this guide

Every walk in this book begins and ends at the same spot. With a single exception they vary in length between 4km and 14km, making them suitable for a morning or afternoon's outing. The exception is Bath's tunnels and canals route which is more of a full day outing, although there's a choice of lunch stops conveniently placed close to the halfway mark. In country areas, public transport is sporadic and, as many people may be arriving by car, postcodes have been included to help find the start. Remember that postcodes are approximate only and the codes given will get you as near to the start as the technology allows.

Although the routes can be generally described as 'moderate', some are tougher than others and a couple involve very steep slopes. Where a route involves any sections of unusually steep ground, it will be mentioned in the notes which precede each walk. The durations given are based on the time it took the authors to walk the route and should be taken as a rough guide only. Similarly, the sketch maps are merely indicative of the route and terrain and should not be relied on for navigation. Having the relevant Ordnance Survey map with you is not only good practice, it can also help interpret your surroundings and, as OS maps show rights of way, allow you to vary or extend the route. Finally, lefts and rights are given according to the direction of travel.

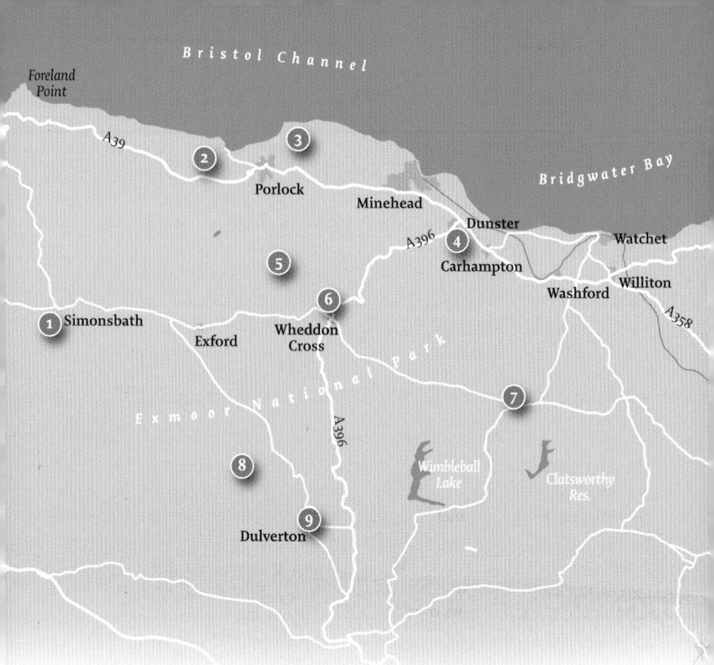

Samuel Taylor Coleridge may have been fuelled by opium when he wrote what is arguably his most famous poem in Exmoor but, for the rest of us, it doesn't take mind-altering drugs to see the beauty of the place. (Okay, *Kubla Khan* wasn't actually about Exmoor, but that's beside the point.) Poets and novelists alike have been inspired by Exmoor's uplands and valleys, woodlands and coastline. Not least, R D Blackmore, whose setting for *Lorna Doone* is now labelled 'Doone Country' on OS maps.

Nearby is the longest and finest coastal woodland in the country; sheltered yet too steep to exploit, it is as close to natural vegetation as you will find in England. Nor is it just the natural world which seems timeless in Exmoor. Dunster has hardly changed from medieval times, Dulverton – the National Park's southern gateway – still relies on vintage road signs to direct people through the town, and locals and visitors still cross rivers on bridges built in the Middle Ages.

Exmoor ponies – Britain's oldest native breed – graze freely on the moors, red deer roam the hills and valleys, stars fill the dark skies, salmon return each year to the River Barle and River Exe to spawn. Time doesn't stand still in Exmoor, but it does seem to pass a little more slowly.

Exmoor

Simonsbath

Distance **11km** Time **3 hours 30**
Terrain **paths, fields and tracks**
Map **OS Explorer OL9** Access **no public transport to the start**

In the 19th century, the government concluded that Exmoor was 'mountainous and cold ground, much beclouded with thick fogges and mists and yielding but a poor kind of turf of little value'. In 1818, it sold the Royal Forest of Exmoor to John Knight, a Midlands industrialist, who set about reclaiming the land for agriculture. Fields were cleared, model farms were built and stone and earth field boundaries were erected, many of which can still be seen today. Simonsbath was the centre of his operations and this walk bears witness to his efforts.

Simonsbath may be the most westerly village in Somerset, but it's certainly not the biggest. It's a 'blink and you'll miss it' cluster of properties on the B3223. Between St Luke's Church and the Exmoor Forest Inn look for a sign directing you into a car park (TA24 7SH). Walk back to the main road and head downhill. At the first road junction, go left towards the river, passing the old sawmill. Just before the bridge, go through a gate on your left to follow the banks of the River Barle as it meanders down through the meadow. After 250m, when you reach a watergate – suspended across the stream to prevent livestock from straying – bear left across the meadow to join a well-established footpath running along the bottom of the hill.

The path follows the unspoilt river valley to the site of a 19th-century mine, one of John Knight's enterprises. Low ruins beside the path are all that remain of the Wheal Eliza copper and iron mine. The miners' accommodation is on the left of the path and the mine shaft is down to the right, behind the fence. After the mine closed in 1857, it hit the headlines when a local widower, William Burgess, used the shaft to dispose of his daughter's body,

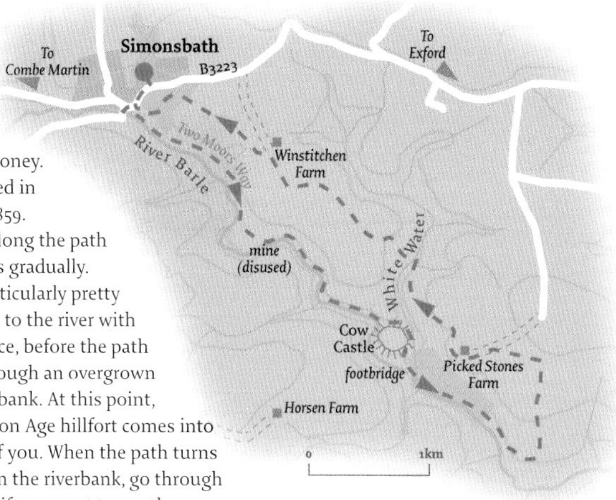

◂ River Barle

after killing her to save money. He was hanged in Taunton in 1859.

Continue along the path as it descends gradually. There is a particularly pretty section, close to the river with a paved surface, before the path turns left through an overgrown beech hedge bank. At this point, Cow Castle Iron Age hillfort comes into view ahead of you. When the path turns left away from the riverbank, go through the gate and, if you want to see the hillfort close up, climb the steep slope to your right. Otherwise, follow the path round the bottom of Cow Castle to cross a small footbridge over White Water and go left on a track.

Continue past (but don't cross) the bigger footbridge at Horsen Ford as you follow the track through the conifer plantation and out onto open ground, with the river to your right. After this, the path passes through gates to moorland. Where the path forks, go left to follow the old boundary of the Royal Forest of Exmoor up the hillside. After 800m, at intersecting paths, turn left and head straight over a field, turning left again on a farm access road.

Signs to Simonsbath lead you round Picked Stones Farm, with the farmyard to your right. Follow the track down into White Water combe, cross the bridge and then head up the fairly steep climb to the top of the hill. Bear left through a gap in the bank and look for the blue marker posts which will lead you along the edge of fields.

The walls beside you, filled with earth and crowned with beech hedging, were part of John Knight's efforts to enclose the land. It is hard not to consider what life was like for the men who built them. When you reach a gate onto the surfaced farm road at Winstitchen Farm, don't go through it but bear left, then follow the blue markers on posts and gates along the field edges. As you enter Birchcleave Wood – which was planted at Knight's instigation and is said to be the highest beech woodland in the country – follow the main track downhill until you emerge back into familiar territory on the road in Simonsbath.

Culbone Church and Woods

Distance 15km Time 5 hours
Terrain paths, tracks (some of them steep) and a short section of quiet road
Map OS Explorer OL9 Access buses from Minehead to Porlock Weir

Culbone Church is said to be the smallest parish church in England. It has a good case for also being the prettiest and possibly the most remote. Culbone is tucked into woodland overlooking the Bristol Channel and is reached by a short but invigorating climb from Porlock Weir, passing through the grounds of a now demolished mansion. The church is worth a visit even if you turn for home thereafter, but this outing goes up onto the high ground, through charming farming country before dropping down for the return leg along the wooded coastal path.

Porlock Weir has a good sized pay & display car park down on the seafront (TA24 8PB). The South West Coast Path is well signposted and sets off behind the hotel, through a gate.

Acorn markers lead through the fields and up to a lane. Turn right and walk up to the arched Toll House at Worthy, leaving it to your left. Soon the long climb begins up a well-defined path, occasionally with steps. Pass below the drive to the demolished Ashley Combe House and then through a tunnel as the path leads uphill.

This was the route used by tradesmen serving the house, so they could come and go without being seen by the occupants. Lord Byron's daughter, Ada, lived in Ashley Combe after her marriage to Lord William King, later the Earl of Lovelace. Ada Lovelace – as she became – was a mathematician who worked with Charles Babbage on the 'analytical engine', an early mechanical computer. Ada's notes, written in the 1830s, gained

◂ Culbone Church

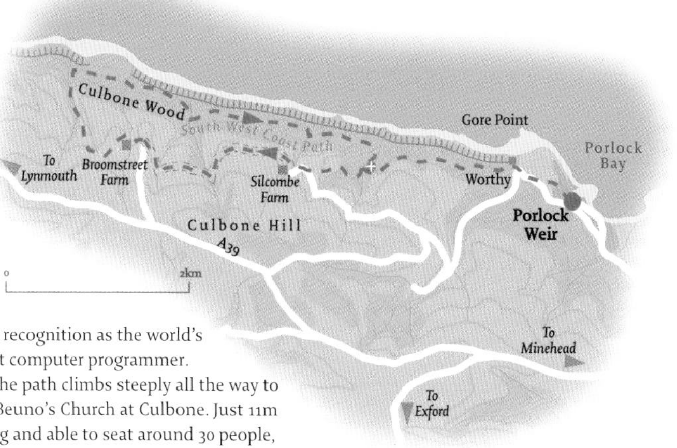

her recognition as the world's first computer programmer.

The path climbs steeply all the way to St Beuno's Church at Culbone. Just 11m long and able to seat around 30 people, this has been a place of Christian worship since before the Norman conquest and is still in regular use today. Take a little gate in the top left corner of the churchyard and turn right to walk under a bridge and past the small gatehouse.

When you join a track, go left and follow it up the hill and over the crest onto the quiet road to Silcombe. Go through the farm and up the track leading round the shoulder of the hill. As you follow the lanes along the hillside, have a look at the hedging on the walls beside you. Hedge 'laying' is a traditional skill that has been practised in this part of the world for centuries. It encourages new growth and re-invigorates an old, overgrown hedge without having to replace it.

Look back when you can for a fine view of Bossington Hill and Hurlstone Point as you follow the track past Broomstreet Farm. When the track opens onto a field by a marker post, turn sharp right to walk downhill, signed to Lynmouth. The path now leads through trees, along a grassy bank and back into woods before dropping down onto a clearly defined path running along the contour.

This is the Coleridge Way, part of the South West Coast Path, where a right turn leads back to Culbone Church. The clean, moist coastal air promotes lush vegetation, from trees and shrubs to ferns, mosses and lichens, all thriving in the damp microclimate. Culbone Wood is often described as Britain's temperate rainforest. The route has been affected by landslips in places but steps have been created to provide safe alternatives.

From the church simply retrace your steps back to the car park at Porlock Weir.

Bossington

Distance 3.5km Time 1 hour 30 Terrain well used paths and tracks Map OS Explorer OL9 Access buses from Porlock Weir and Minehead stop at Allerford, a 10-minute walk along quiet lanes from Bossington

The old coastguard lookout tower which commands the headland over Hurlstone Point makes a great target for the outward leg of this coastal walk. There are views over the Bristol Channel to Wales on a clear day and the outlook is just as good over Porlock Bay on the way back. Bossington village is a little Somerset delight: thatched cottages, fancy chimney stacks, and trim gardens line the street. To cap it all, there's a picturesque tearoom waiting at the end.

The roads leading to Bossington from the A39 are narrow, so proceed with caution to reach the National Trust car park in the middle of the village (TA24 8HQ). It is just past the Kitnors Tearoom and payment is required to park (free for National Trust members).

Cross the footbridge close to the entrance and turn left to follow a track under the trees to a farm gate. Take a path which forks right, heading gently uphill with the rugged rocks of Hurlstone Point and the outline of the coastguard station ahead. Go past the NT marker and bench on a path which narrows as it climbs.

The tower, reached by a flight of steps, was built in 1902. It housed a rocket warning system and rescue equipment with a semaphore signalling post nearby. The station ceased to be staffed after World War II and closed in 1983. Now a shell, it makes a magnificent viewpoint with a wide panorama stretching from the Severn estuary to your right, to South Wales across the Bristol Channel, and left over the Somerset coastline as far as Foreland Point in Devon.

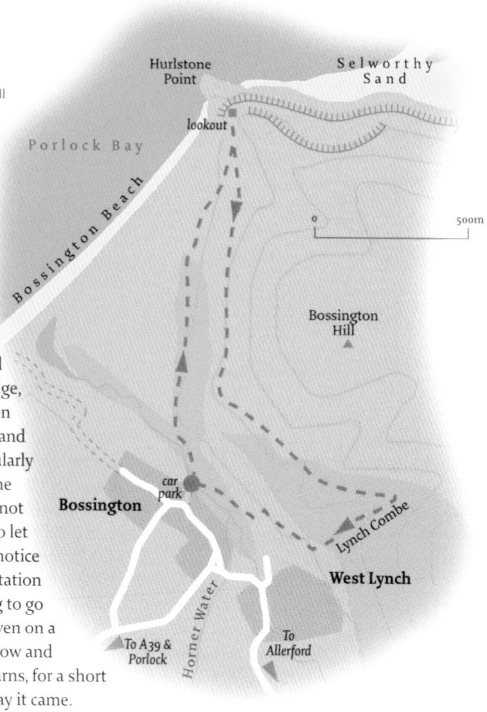

◂ Porlock Bay from Bossington Hill

Some 8000 years ago the stretch of water between north Somerset and Wales didn't exist. The two coasts were separated only by marshland which gradually succumbed to the sea and became the Bristol Channel. Even today the coastline is still changing. The shingle ridge, which protects Bossington Beach, is being breached and the fields behind are regularly flooded with seawater. The authorities have decided not to repair the breach but to let nature take its course. A notice on the path beyond the station warns against attempting to go further in bad weather. Even on a good day, the path is narrow and exposed so the route returns, for a short distance only, back the way it came.

After savouring the views, go down the hill for 100m and fork left by an old metal post. The path now climbs gently round the side of the hill with the shingle beach of Porlock Bay down to the right. Ignore the path heading steeply uphill to the left and continue to walk round the hill with charming views over the fields and lanes far below. When the path starts to descend into trees, don't take the path leading right (signed to Bossington) but carry on round the hillside with a stout stone wall down to your right. Cross the wall via a wooden gate and continue down through the woods. After the next gate, follow the path round to the right. Go right on joining a wide path at the bottom and walk across the field to the far side. Stepping into the next field, a yellow marker directs you left. The path leads into woodlands and bends to the right, continuing back to the footbridge beside the car park.

Dunster

Distance 5km Time 2 hours
Terrain woodland tracks and paths
Map OS Explorer OL9 Access buses from Dulverton & Minehead stop in Dunster. West Somerset Railway operates to Dunster Station which is an easy 2km walk from the start

With its picturesque streets and dramatic castle, Dunster is one of the prettiest villages in all of Somerset, and probably one of the most visited. Almost unchanged since medieval times, it can be very busy in the height of the season, but cross the famous Gallox Bridge and the crowds are soon left behind. Ahead lie verdant woodlands, ancient remains, wonderful views and, if you're lucky, a close encounter with Exmoor ponies.

Arriving by steam train at the delightfully nostalgic Dunster Station is a great way to start the walk, although it adds around 25 minutes at the beginning (and end, if returning to the station). Steam trains run between Bishop's Lydeard and Minehead on England's longest 'heritage railway'. The West Somerset Railway has just over 32km of track, all restored, staffed and maintained by volunteers. A noticeboard outside the station shows the way to reach the start of the walk. If arriving by car, use the pay & display car park on the left-hand side shortly after leaving the A39 (TA24 6SE).

Walk uphill to the top of the car park to join the pavement beside the main road, following it round into the village. Standing at the top of the High Street, over 3km from the sea, it's strange to think that in the 12th century Dunster sat on the coast and prospered as a port for Exmoor. Even in medieval times, when the sea had receded, Dunster thrived as a centre for the woollen trade, leading to the construction of the distinctive Yarn Market at the turn of the 16th century.

On reaching the traffic lights, continue ahead up Castle Hill, soon bearing right to

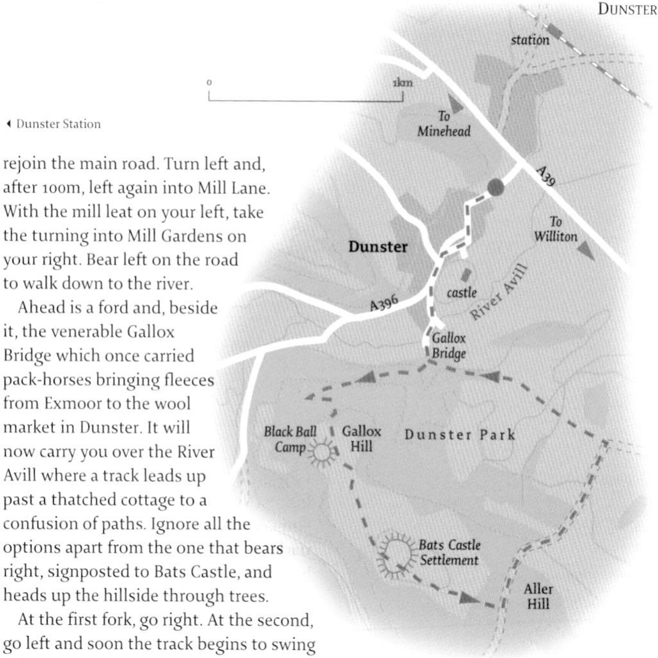

rejoin the main road. Turn left and, after 100m, left again into Mill Lane. With the mill leat on your left, take the turning into Mill Gardens on your right. Bear left on the road to walk down to the river.

Ahead is a ford and, beside it, the venerable Gallox Bridge which once carried pack-horses bringing fleeces from Exmoor to the wool market in Dunster. It will now carry you over the River Avill where a track leads up past a thatched cottage to a confusion of paths. Ignore all the options apart from the one that bears right, signposted to Bats Castle, and heads up the hillside through trees.

At the first fork, go right. At the second, go left and soon the track begins to swing left. When it levels out, with a viewpoint to the right, go left until you are able to take a track which cuts back left and climbs by a marker pointing to the Deer Park circuit. (Ignore the Bats Castle marker at this point.) The path leads uphill and bends right through a wooden palisade to continue up the hill. Soon the path opens onto the hilltop with the earthworks of the prehistoric hillfort to the right, known as Black Ball Camp.

A little further and the path passes through the second and higher prehistoric settlement of Bats Castle. The views from here are spectacular, including the one behind, looking over the fields and valley to the high moor beyond. Keep on the same compass bearing to walk over the grass, through a gate and into the woods via a gate in a wooden palisade. Turn left and walk down the ancient byway towards the bottom of the hill until the main path bears right, beside a marker post. Take the path which heads through a gate to the left, signed to Dunster. It leads along a fence with the castle over to the right, before dropping down to a gate and onto a track. Turn right to cross the Gallox Bridge and walk back into the village.

Dunkery Hill

Distance **7km** Time **3 hours**
Terrain **woodland paths, tracks and footpaths** Map **OS Explorer OL9**
Access **no public transport to the start**

The Beacon on Dunkery Hill is the highest point in Somerset and an easy walk from the car park. If you just want to enjoy the view, head up the path to the top. On the other hand, if you want to turn the walk into a bit of an adventure, set off downhill in the opposite direction. You might get strange looks from tourists in the car park, but they're the ones missing out on this lovely woodland walk – topped off with 360-degree views from the summit.

A minor road from Wheddon Cross to Luccombe runs across the moorland some 120m from the summit and passes two convenient places to park. This walk sets off from the lower of the two car parks, at Dunkery Gate.

Although the road from Luccombe passes through the car park, if arriving from Wheddon Cross don't be tempted to turn left where a road sign shows it is a dead end. Instead, continue ahead and park just after crossing a cattle grid (TA24 7AT).

From the car park, face the cattle grid and take the path which sets off left, signed to Blagdon Wood. It leads through a gate and across a field to another gate. Immediately on the left, a third gate allows you into the woods. It's now a gentle walk downhill on a clear but little used path that rises and falls, going back into a field for a short stretch and then returning to the woods, all the time with the River Avill below to the left. Follow the path all the way down, rounding a corner (where you may have to share the route with a stream for a few metres) before starting to climb again.

On joining another path – the Coleridge Way – go left for about 50 paces before turning left again, signed to Dunkery

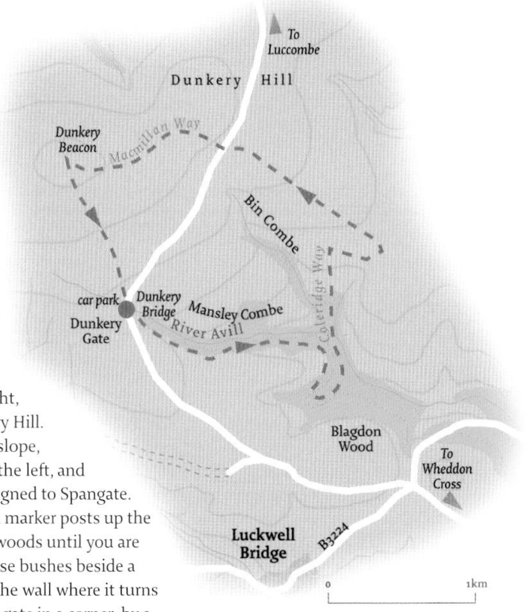

◂ On Dunkery Hill

Beacon, to walk down the side of the hill. Turn left at the water's edge to walk upstream and pass through a wooden gate. Cross the river to your right, heading for Dunkery Hill.

Continue up the slope, ignoring a path on the left, and take a bridlepath, signed to Spangate. Follow blue-topped marker posts up the hill and out of the woods until you are walking among gorse bushes beside a stone wall. Follow the wall where it turns right and leads to a gate in a corner, by a marker post. Bear left to climb uphill again, now with a fence to your right.

At the crest of the hill, look for a track which sets off through the heather to the left, heading in the direction of Dunkery Beacon, with a solitary marker post near the start for reassurance. Follow the track to cross a road, and strike out over the heather, generally aiming in the same direction. Soon you will come to a wide stone pathway which crosses the path. This is the Macmillan Way which runs all the way from Lincolnshire to Dorset. Follow it to the left to the top of Dunkery Hill.

At 520m above sea level, Dunkery Hill is the second highest point in the south of England (after Dartmoor). The hill and surrounding land was given in stages to the National Trust by various donors, and in 1935 a plaque was erected into the summit cairn. On a clear day you can see almost 150km – there's a useful topograph close to the cairn to point out the highlights.

Paths lead off from the summit in all directions, but the one you want is to your left as you face the plaque on the cairn. Follow it down the hill and back to the cattle grid at Dunkery Gate.

Snowdrop Valley

Distance **5km** Time **2 hours**
Terrain **paths, tracks and quiet country roads** Map **OS Explorer OL9** Access **buses from Minehead and Dulverton**

For many years, this little valley in the middle of Exmoor with its annual carpet of snowdrops was a hidden gem, a secret known only to the locals. As word spread, the number of visitors increased, and for the last 20 years a peak-season Park & Ride system has been operating to reduce congestion in the narrow lane. The village and the valley are busy when the snowdrops are out – usually around February – but this walk is still full of interest even when the *Galanthus Nivalis* have gone.

Wheddon Cross, the highest village on Exmoor, grew up around the crossroads created when a turnpike was built between Minehead and Bampton in the 19th century. With its smaller but older neighbour Cutcombe, it retains many services lost to other villages like a shop, garage, school, church, pub and post office. It also has a livestock market to cement its importance to the surrounding agricultural community. There is a public car park beside the Rest and Be Thankful Inn which sits on the crossroads (TA24 7DR).

Walk up to the car park entrance between the pub and a bus shelter and cross the busy A396. Turn left and follow the pavement, over the crossroads and down to the war memorial. Bear right to the school, then follow the road signposted to Cutcombe. Where the road bends right, take a footpath on the left to walk down through a gate and across a field. Go straight across the main road and down a track to farm buildings. After 90m, join a little path on the right, signposted to Drapers Way.

The path leads through the trees on the side of a valley. Go right where it forks

◂ Sign for Wheddon Cross

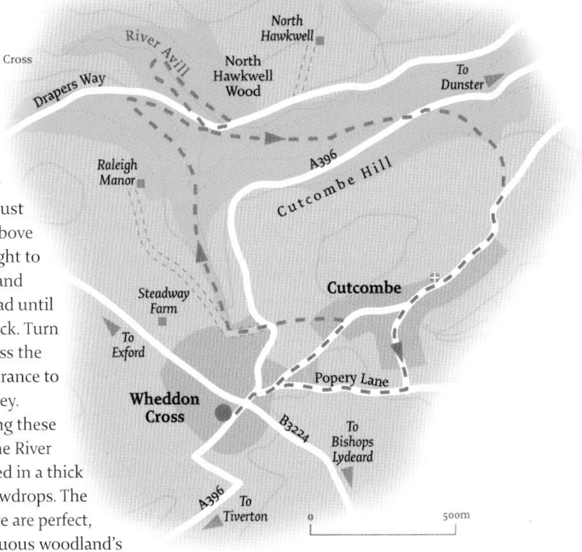

to continue downhill until it is crossed by another path, just a few metres above a road. Turn right to walk beside – and above – the road until you reach a track. Turn left here to cross the road at the entrance to Snowdrop Valley.

In early spring these banks along the River Avill are covered in a thick blanket of snowdrops. The conditions here are perfect, with the deciduous woodland's shaded, nutrient-rich soil. In years gone by, snowdrops from the valley were harvested and sold commercially in Minehead but now it is against the law to pick them. Around 10,000 people visit each year, but avoid the snowdrop season and you are likely to have the place to yourself.

Go through the gate and follow the path beside the stream until you can cross over a footbridge. Now the path leads down the other side of the river back to the road. Turn right and walk 100m until you can turn left, back up the track opposite the Snowdrop Valley entrance gate. After a few steps, bear left and follow the track as it gradually climbs through the woods, gently gaining height. Ignore a path which crosses your route, but take the next little trail which forks to the right to climb up a slightly sunken pathway to reach a road.

Cross with care, then take the track opposite which leads through a conifer plantation and, after getting gradually steeper, opens into a field. Follow the left-hand field edge to a gate at the top of the hill. Turn left to reach a road, and then right to walk along it. After passing a church, take the left fork and follow the lane out of the village and uphill, bending right at the crossroads at the top. Popery Lane now runs back to the school, where a left turn leads into Wheddon Cross. If visiting in 'snowdrop season', the villagers are probably serving teas in Moorland Hall, which is 50m beyond the car park along the main road.

The Brendon Hill Incline

Distance **7km** Time **3 hours**
Terrain **paths, lanes and fields; the route begins with a long steep descent and ends with a shorter but equally steep ascent** Map **OS Explorer OL9**
Access **no public transport to the start**

As the title suggests, this walk involves a very steep hill but, for the most part, you are going downhill. 'The Incline' was built to lower wagons of iron ore from the Brendon Hills mines to the West Somerset Mineral Railway line below. Its construction, in 1861, remains testament to human ingenuity, particularly when there's a profit to be made (although in this case there wasn't). The walk is straight - literally straight - downhill for the first 1km before it heads off for a charming meander through lanes and fields until the gentle return uphill - gentle that is, but for the last 400m. You have been warned!

There's a small parking area 1.5km west of Ralegh's Cross, just beside the railway bridge buttresses at the top of The Incline (TA23 0LL). Set off through the gate where you will immediately see the Winding House on your right.

Here huge drums controlled cables which lowered wagons full of iron ore down the 1:4 slope. It took about 12 minutes to get from the top to Comberow at the bottom and the weight of the heavy wagons going down pulled the empty ones up; it was entirely self powered. Passengers were allowed to ride the wagons 'free and at their own risk'!

Head straight down the slope, sometimes on an embankment, sometimes in a cutting - at one point the track bed is held up by a high retaining wall, now protected behind safety railings. At the bottom of the hill, descend the stairs before bearing right into Comberow. Look for a marker post which directs you to 'Roadwater' and a path which sets off

◂ Brendon Hill Incline

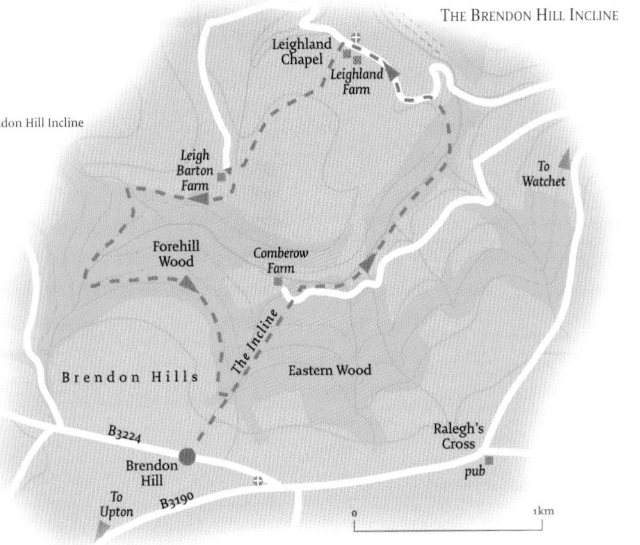

between hedges, soon to follow the route along which the railway line once carried ore to the coast at Watchet.

When a path joins from the right, head left, crossing two footbridges (or wading through the ford) before setting off up the hillside, leaving a house down to the right. Pass through a small orchard at the top and bear left when you reach a road. This leads to a church, opposite which the path turns left. Keep to the left edge of a paddock to go through a gate at the top. Turn right into a field. Now make for the gate up the slope to your left, going straight across the field.

After the next gate, bear half right to walk round the shoulder of the hill and join a track to Leigh Barton Farm. Go through a gate on the right to pass a duck pond to the farm buildings. Go left before bearing right to make your way round the back of the farmyard to a farm gate with a marker post. Take the middle route, signposted to 'The Incline', keeping right just after the gate.

Dropping downhill, ignore the next sign to 'The Incline' and walk past a little house, following the path round the bend and up the other side of the combe. This path joins a track and leads past a waterfall. Soon after, take the path on the right for the long but not too steep walk up the hillside. After climbing for 1km, the path bends sharply left and heads steeply downhill. After a few metres, a path on the right leads back onto The Incline. Your car is 400m in a straight line up to your right. Sorry!

The Tarr Steps

Distance **13km** Time **4 hours**
Terrain **paths and country roads**
Map **OS Explorer OL9**
Access **no public transport**

People have been crossing the River Barle by the Tarr Steps for hundreds of years. No-one is sure when the slabs of stone were first hauled into place – the bridge is possibly medieval and probably older – but in recent times it has been washed away so often the stones have been numbered to make them easier to reassemble. This old bridge is one of Somerset's treasures and marks the starting point for a sublime walk along the riverbank. It's also the finishing point for the return leg over the moor.

Park in the official Tarr Steps Car Park, some 700m west of Liscombe Farm (TA22 9QA). There is a modest charge for the day. Set off down the surfaced path by the vehicle exit and continue downhill when you join a road. At the bottom is the River Barle and the famous crossing.

The Tarr Steps is a monster of a 'clapper' bridge, the longest crossing of its kind (and arguably the oldest working bridge of its type in the country), with huge slabs of stone weighing up to two tons each resting on massive boulders. On the far side, turn sharp right to put the river by your right hand. Most walkers will be on the opposite bank at this point, but they miss a lovely path which affords good views over the water.

The Barle is an Exmoor river from its source until it merges with the Exe just south of Dulverton. Look out for the wire cable slung across the water. It has been put there to catch debris in the floods and save the Tarr Steps from further damage.

◂ The Tarr Steps

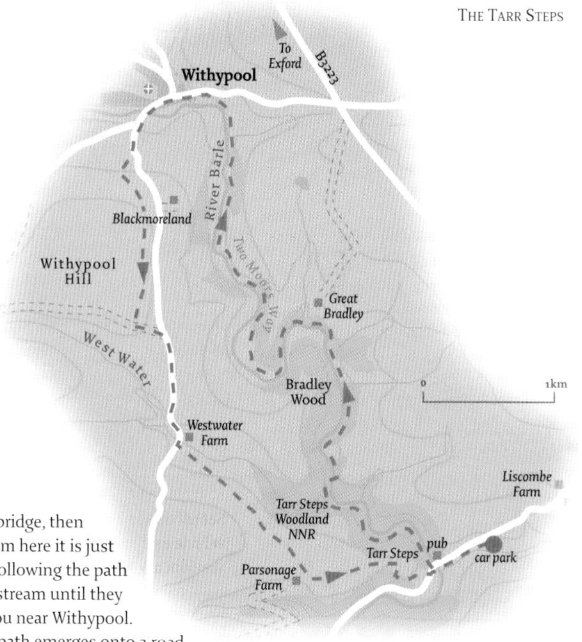

Cross a footbridge, then turn left. From here it is just a matter of following the path and river upstream until they diverge as you near Withypool.

When the path emerges onto a road, turn left to reach the village, which gets its name from the withies (willow trees) that grow along the bank. The village provides all the services you need at the halfway mark, with a pub, village shop and a tearoom in the old filling station. Fork left to cross the river – the six-arched bridge is only 100 years old – then head up the road on the other side. It's fairly steep and although the road is quiet, you might prefer to step onto the moor by the village hall car park.

Keep left as you climb until you are walking parallel to the road. In time the route is barred by a field enclosure, at which point bear left to join the road by a cattle grid. Now turn right and walk down to the bottom of the valley by Westwater Farm. Cross a little bridge and go left into a field where a sign points to Tarr Steps. Follow the path across fields, generally heading in a straight line to reach Parsonage Farm. Turn left and walk over the brow and down the other side; at the corner of the field (with two farm gates), go right down a sunken track. One more left turn and you are back at Tarr Steps.

It's a lot of ups and downs on the return leg and once you've reached the river it's back uphill to the car park.

Dulverton

Distance **6.5km** Time **2 hours 30** Terrain **woodland paths, tracks and fields** Map **OS Explorer OL9 or 114** Access **buses from Minehead, Tiverton and Taunton**

Dulverton – the 'southern gateway to Exmoor' – is an historic little market town, tucked in a wooded valley near the confluence of the Rivers Barle and Exe. The place is full of character with antiquated road signs, independent shops and a charming town hall. There's much to explore in the town itself before setting off into the countryside that surrounds it.

Roadside parking is at a premium in Dulverton, but the off-street car parks are well signposted from the main road (TA22 9EX). Head for the centre of town and, if you have time, pop into the National Park Centre which is full of interesting information about Exmoor and Dulverton.

As you walk uphill, the town hall with its distinctive double external stairway and elevated porch is to your right. Originally the market house, it was converted to a town hall in 1866, although the stairs and porch date from 1930. Go ahead into Bank Square, bearing right at the top up the side of the churchyard. At the corner of the church, turn right along Church Lane, with its rustic cobbling underfoot, then climb uphill towards the Rock House Inn.

Leave the thatched house to your right and turn into School Lane, bending first to the left past an old mill, then right by the gates to the former school, now a private house. An ancient track leads up through the woods for over 500m, gaining height steadily. Ignore a path heading left and follow the main route, going past white gateposts before bearing round to the right beside a line of beech trees.

At a three-way fingerpost, go right on a path, signed to Court Down, which initially

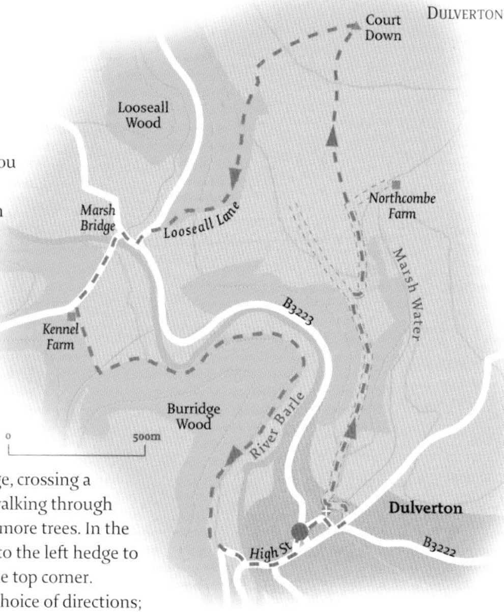

bends back the way you came, before turning sharp left. Go through a gate to a marker post leading into a field. Aim for the far right-hand corner, where a track leads into the next field, overlooking Northcombe Farm.

As the track bends downhill, keep left to follow the field edge, crossing a farm track and then walking through a copse of young sycamore trees. In the next field, stick close to the left hedge to reach a field gate at the top corner. A fingerpost offers a choice of directions; head for 'Broford Farm' and the trig point will soon appear over the brow.

From the high point of this walk, turn back to face the way you have come, then bear right to walk to a gap in the hedge between two tall spindly trees. Follow the sign to 'Marsh Bridge', keeping to the left-hand side of the field as you make your way downhill, with a picturesque patchwork of fields on the hemispherical hill opposite.

A gate in the corner opens onto a track. Follow this for a short distance to a marker post, then turn right on a path known as Looseall Lane (although it is signed for Marsh Bridge) and follow it downhill, keeping right at the fork. Cross the roads at the bottom to a stone bridge, then head over the painted iron bridge beyond. Carry on past a tearoom and, 250m further on, join a path to Dulverton on the left.

Pass through Kennel Farm and into woods. Keep left, resisting any temptation to head uphill to the right. The path joins the River Barle for a time before the two became separated by a meadow as they follow a parallel course down the valley. Every now and then there are tantalising glimpses of Dulverton across the valley. The woodland path becomes a narrow lane beside Horner Cottage and leads down to a road. Turn left and left again over the bridge to walk back into Dulverton.

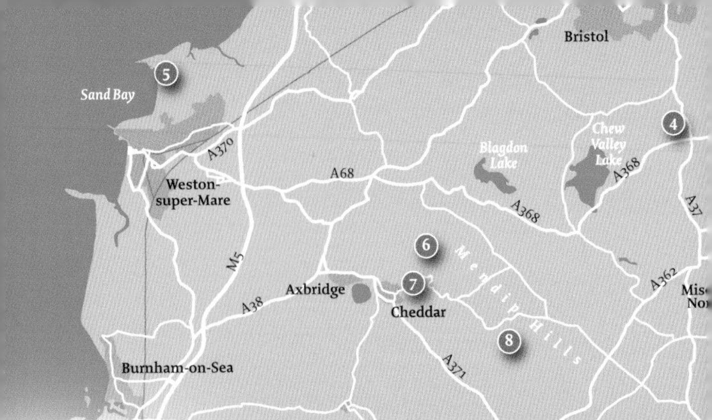

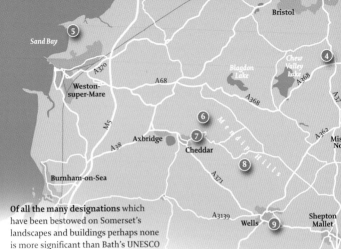

Of all the many designations which have been bestowed on Somerset's landscapes and buildings perhaps none is more significant than Bath's UNESCO World Heritage Site status. Roman baths, the Royal Crescent and Pulteney Bridge are the highlights of a city which is nothing less than an architectural wonderland. And it's small enough to be explored on foot.

Close by are hidden legacies of the Industrial Revolution – mills, mines and canals – which have been mellowed by the passing of time and now add to the tapestry of interest in the surrounding countryside. To the south lie the Mendips, a range of limestone hills stretching from the Victorian seaside resort of Weston-super-Mare to the historic market town of Frome, close to the Wiltshire border. Once mined for lead and silver, the hills are punctuated by deep gorges and rocky outcrops, most famously Cheddar Gorge. And being limestone, underground rivers have carved out spectacular caverns, like Gough's Cave and Wookey Hole, both now major tourist attractions. Not far away is Wells, which is technically a city but with the atmosphere of a village, albeit a village with a stunning cathedral, an extraordinary clock and a street which has been occupied since the 14th century.

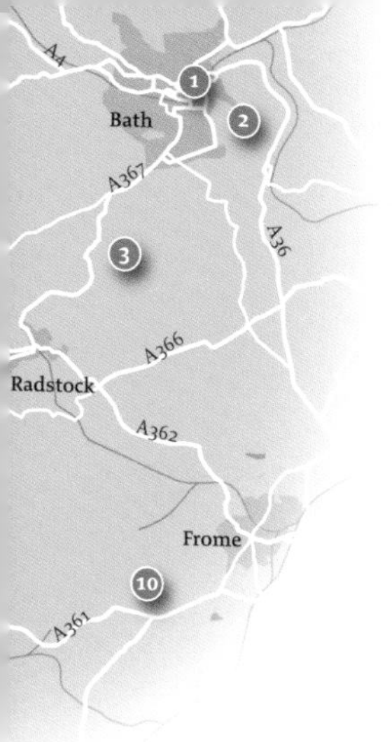

The Mendips and Bath

Bath and Bathwick Hill

Distance 4km **Time** 1 hour 30
Terrain pavements and paths
Map OS Explorer 155 **Access** Bath is well served by trains and buses. If coming by car, use one of the three Park & Ride facilities to avoid the challenge of parking in the centre

'Oh! Who can ever be tired of Bath?' asked Jane Austen's heroine Catherine Morland. Two centuries after she wrote *Northanger Abbey*, it's still hard to imagine growing weary of the place. In its Georgian heyday, gentlemen and gentlewomen would 'take the air' by strolling through the pleasure gardens to the meadows on Bathwick Hill. This route, devised by the National Trust, follows in their footsteps.

When Edgar the Peaceful was crowned King of England in Bath Abbey in 973 – in a service which forms the basis of the present-day British coronation ceremony – the place looked a little different. It has been derelict twice in its long history and the present Gothic building was only created in the 19th century. The walk starts from the abbey's west door, with three Coats of Arms carved into the wood, and bears right to cross the square in front of Bath's tourist information centre.

Go left along York Street and use the pedestrian crossings to reach the balustrades overlooking Parade Gardens, once an orchard tended by monks and converted to formal gardens in the 18th century. Walk with the river to your right, and a good view of Robert Adam's Pulteney Bridge ahead. Cross the bridge – England's answer to Ponte Vecchio in Florence – then continue up Great Pulteney Street, where Austen set *Northanger Abbey*.

For a time 36 Great Pulteney Street was home to the anti-slavery campaigner William Wilberforce, whose house is

◂ The Kennet & Avon Canal

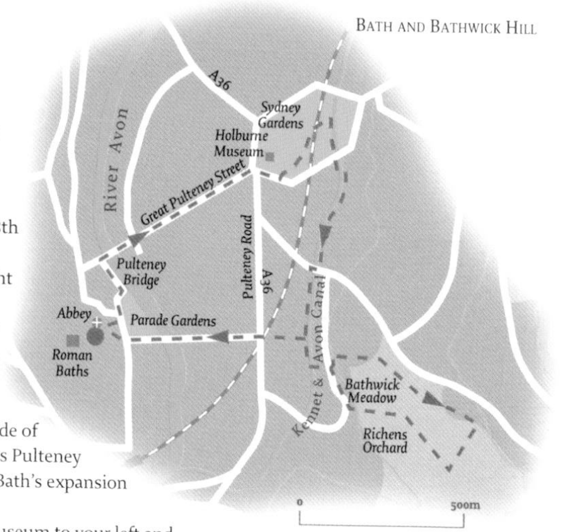

marked with a commemorative plaque. In the late 18th century, Sir William Pulteney was thought to be the wealthiest man in Britain, after marrying an heiress. Her inheritance included Bathwick Estate, on the east side of the River Avon. It was Pulteney who largely funded Bath's expansion across the river.

Leave Holburne Museum to your left and walk up the pavement to enter Sydney Gardens behind the museum. Bear left until you can turn right onto a wide path leading past a pillared folly and across a bridge over the railway. Turn right just before the next bridge, looking for a white iron gateway which leads onto the Kennet & Avon Canal towpath.

Turn right and, after passing through a tunnel, go up the steps (or ramp) to cross the canal and continue along the other side. At the boat basin, the towpath climbs a cobbled ramp to join the road. Cross with care, then turn right to find steps beside the supermarket leading back to the towpath. On reaching a lock, go over the canal bridge to cross a street called Sydney Buildings, continuing up steps on the other side.

For the next 500m, follow the path up the side of Bathwick Fields, ignoring gates in the metal fence, until you reach a bench at the top. It's a good place to stop for a breather and to admire the view back over Bath. Behind the bench, go through a gate on the right and walk downhill for 150m until you can cross a stile on your right.

The path now runs straight out across the grass, to pass through three gates beside Richens Orchard. After the third, continue across the hillside for 80m where a left turn, in a dip, will take you to a gate back into Sydney Buildings. Turn right to go back down the lane to re-cross the canal, then turn right on the towpath for 80m until you can descend to steps on the left. Continue downhill, passing under a railway bridge to Pulteney Road. Cross into North Parade to walk back across the river. Turn right on Pierrepont Street and you will see the Abbey across the road to your left.

Bath's tunnels and canals

Distance **20km** Time **6 hours**
Terrain **surfaced paths and two sections of public road** Map **OS Explorer 155**
Access **buses and trains to Bath**

There are not many places you can walk underground safely in this country, and only one where you can do it for 1600m. Almost £2 million was invested to turn a disused railway line – complete with two tunnels and a viaduct – into a 'greenway' which has become a popular route for walkers and cyclists alike. When linked with the Kennet & Avon Canal towpath, it makes for a memorable outing. Whatever the weather, it can be a little chilly in the tunnels – it's also sensible to carry a torch.

Modern traffic does little to enhance the beauty of Bath, but three strategically placed Park & Ride facilities make it easy to visit the city without adding to the congestion or worrying about parking. The service from Odd Down (BA2 8AL) operates to St James's Parade, where the walk begins. Head down the street in the direction of the bus station's distinctive glass and metal rotunda, bearing right and crossing the road when it's safe.

Go right on the pavement beside the River Avon until you can take the path down to the riverside. With the water on your left, follow the river for 2km, passing under several bridges along the way. Some 400m beyond a heavy railway bridge, cross the river on Weston footbridge. Walk past the supermarket, turning left on the main road for 100m. Cross into Burnham Road, then bear left into Inverness Road. Turn right onto the greenway which is accessed from the end of the street.

From now on you are likely to be sharing the path with cyclists so keep your wits about you. The first tunnel, the Devonshire, is 409m – a taster for the longer one to come. The tunnels are dimly lit, but it is a good idea to stand aside for cyclists or to carry a torch to make sure you can be seen. The second stretch underground is the 1600m Combe Down

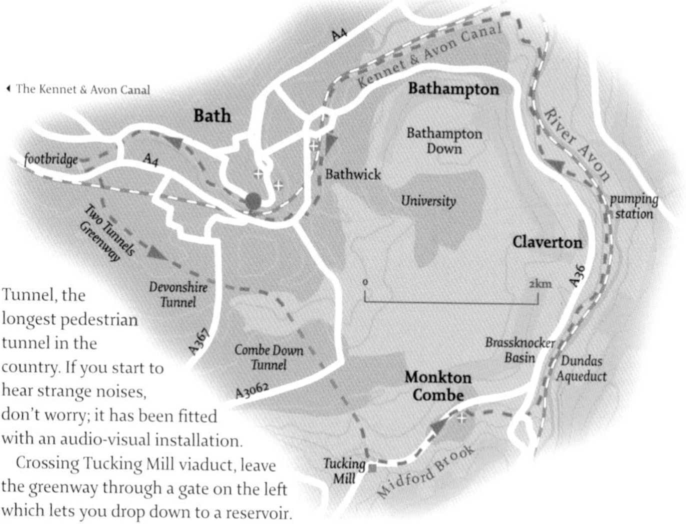

◂ The Kennet & Avon Canal

Tunnel, the longest pedestrian tunnel in the country. If you start to hear strange noises, don't worry; it has been fitted with an audio-visual installation.

Crossing Tucking Mill viaduct, leave the greenway through a gate on the left which lets you drop down to a reservoir. Turn right to walk to a road and then head left to Monkton Combe. Follow the road through the village and then turn right after the last school building. Drop downhill, initially with the school close to your right hand, to pass the front door of the Sports Centre. Turn left on reaching a road and left again after passing under a roadbridge. This leads to the surviving section of the Somerset Coal Canal at Brassknocker Basin.

Walk through the car park, or up on the towpath, until you can see the splendid Dundas Aqueduct on your right. It carries the Kennet & Avon Canal over the River Avon and while you should walk out to see it, our path lies to the left to cross the canal, where you turn right and then re-cross the canal to join the towpath. For the next 7.5km simply follow the towpath, with the canal on your left.

Once back among the buildings of Bath, the towpath passes through two short tunnels before crossing to the other side of the canal for 300m. On crossing back, via the roadbridge at Bathwick Hill, the steps back down to the towpath are found beside the supermarket on the other side of the road. Where the towpath appears to end at a busy road (with '8/9' painted on the lock gate arm), turn left without crossing the carriageway, then left again down steps back to the water's edge.

The canal joins the River Avon at the next lock, but the path continues along the riverside, passing under two bridges, before allowing you to cross the river to the rotunda at the end of St James's Parade.

Combe Hay

Distance **10km** Time **3 hours 30**
Terrain **paths, fields and quiet roads**
Map **OS Explorer 155** Access **buses from Bath to Odd Down every 15 minutes**

There's not much to see of the old Somerset Coal Canal these days, but in the 19th century it was something to behold. Just 10 miles long, it required 23 locks, two aqueducts and a tunnel to traverse the undulating terrain, as well as an innovative – but nearly catastrophic – lock design. Much of the route was later used for a railway which, with the tracks now gone, enthusiasts hope some day to restore. Until then, the few visible remains hint at the industrial past of today's tranquil valley.

There's no problem finding a parking space for this walk. The huge Odd Down Park & Ride terminus on the A367 is free, unless you buy a bus ticket into town (BA2 2AL). Head back through the main entrance, following the pavement round to the right into Combe Hay Lane.

After 400m, where the lane forks, go through a kissing gate on the right to join a path along the top of the woods – it can get a bit overgrown – until you find yourself walking along the top of rough pasture with the valley to your left. Maintain height as you draw near the A367 to pass through a gate opening onto a track bearing left, away from the road.

This is part of the Fosse Way, built by the Romans 2000 years ago, linking Exeter to Lincoln. Follow its course, crossing a quiet public road on the way, until it ends with a sharp turn down to the main road. Take care crossing to a bus stop, before turning left to walk downhill. Pass a cricket pitch on the right, cross back over the carriageway and look for a low threshold by the start of a handrail. This leads down steep steps to the banks of the Cam Brook.

Stay close to the stream as it meanders

◂ Meadow near Combe Hay

along the valley, passing through three fields to reach a road. Cross and continue along the bottom of the next field until you can bear left up into trees, where a path leads to a gate onto a road. Turn right and walk through Combe Hay, keeping right at the fork before following the road as it bends left and right and out of the village.

Not long after the Wheatsheaf pub, take a path which begins in the fork of the road and follow it through trees to a bridge. Before continuing, take a moment to read the information board attached to the brickwork. It tells the story of the canal and the alarming attempt to build a 'caisson lock' to transfer barges between the low and high ground. This involved sealing the barge in a watertight box and then sinking it in a column of water. The scheme came unstuck when trustees and investors were nearly asphyxiated when they took a ride in it. The idea was swiftly dropped in favour of an inclined plane, then later the flight of 22 locks, some of which lie ahead.

Walk under the bridge and up past the locks. Ignore any paths departing left and follow the main track up the valley until you can bear right up a field to pass through a gate by a row of cottages. The path continues uphill beside the fence and then bears left across a field to a concrete track. Follow it left to a viewpoint and continue along the shoulder of the hill. When the track goes right, continue ahead on a path for 350m, turning right when faced with a wooden kissing gate. Follow the fence back to Combe Hay Lane where a right turn leads back to the start of the walk.

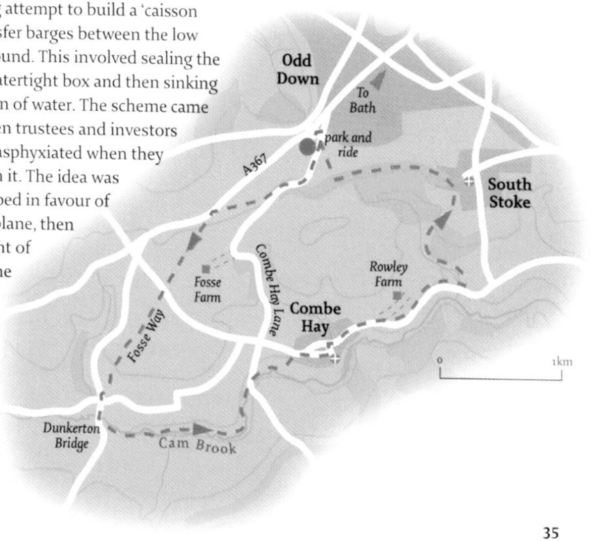

Stanton Drew

Distance **6km** Time **2 hours**
Terrain **fields and tracks**
Map **OS Explorer 155**
Access **buses from Blagdon and Broadmead stop by the Druids Arms**

Stanton Drew's standing stones make up one of the largest collections of monoliths in England, yet for some reason they are also among the least known. The three circles (for which a very modest admission fee is payable) sit in a field just outside the village while three standing stones, called 'The Cove', can be found in the beer garden of the local pub. They provide bookends for this charming walk along the River Chew to Pensford.

Although there are a couple of parking spaces close to the stone circles, they are intended for people visiting the stones. Instead, use the parking area beside the road just beyond the Druid's Arms pub (BS39 4JP).

Leave the pub to your right as you walk into the village, turning into the first road on the right and following it round to pass a postbox. At the end of a high wall, a gate beside a farm road marks the start of the route. To see the stones close up, take the road on the left where you'll find the entrance to the circles.

The Great Circle is more than 100m wide and stands in farmland seemingly strewn randomly with massive lumps of sandstone, breccia and limestone. Local legend has it that the stones are the remains of a wedding party held on the sabbath. The guests were lured by the only musician who'd play on a Sunday – the Devil in disguise – and turned to stone for their sins.

Return out of the gate and back to the start of the walk, passing through the foot gate to follow the farm road past the buildings. After going through two gates, a path begins beside a track, bearing gently

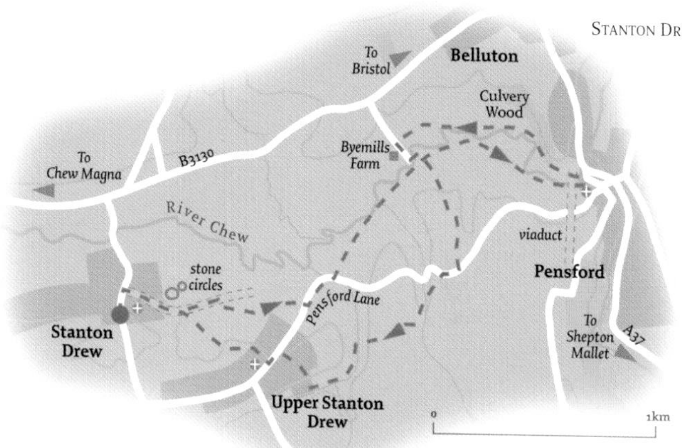

right to a gap in the hedge. Continue the same line across the next two fields, rounding the end of a line of apple trees in the second, before crossing a road. Bear left on a path that follows the hedge to rejoin the road. Cross and continue beside the hedge in the next field to a gate, where you bear left again to follow the river to the house and weir at Byemills.

Leave the house and its garden wall to your left and follow the path as it leads towards the viaduct at Pensford. The rails were lifted after the great flood of 1968 when the viaduct was deemed unsafe for use. Keep to the left to pass under the arch, then bear left to cross an old bridge over a weir. Walk up behind the Rising Sun pub to the village.

Church Street, down to your right, is worth wandering along, but our route takes us round the building to the left. As you pass, don't miss the plaque above head height which shows the flood level in 1968. Turn left up a narrow road, back under the viaduct and into Culvery Wood. After 100m, go left through a gate onto a path leading through fields to a road beside a house. Turn left and follow the road until it crosses the earlier path by the cottage at Byemills. Go straight ahead and uphill, walking between hedges to Pensford Lane.

Turn right and after 60m take a path into the field on the left. Aim for the top left corner where a footbridge leads into the next field. Bear left to a gate, then keep the hedge close to your right until you pass through two gates in quick succession. Now keep the hedge close to your left to reach a lane. Turn right to head into Upper Stanton Drew, forking left to the junction with Pensford Lane. Join the footpath on the other side behind a handrail, turning right after 20m to walk up beside a house and along the side of a field to a gate. Turn left to the next gate. Now head diagonally across to the far corner where stone steps and a gate lead through the hedge. From there it's easy to retrace your steps into the village.

◂ Stanton Drew standing stones

Sand Point and Middle Hope

Distance **7.5km** Time **2 hours**
Terrain **fields and paths**
Map **OS Explorer 153** Access **buses from Weston-super-Mare to Sand Bay**

The coastline between Sand Point and St Thomas's Head is quite unlike the landscape around it. Just up the coast from the bustling seaside resort of Weston-super-Mare, it's an outpost of the Mendip Hills, jutting out into the estuary like an anvil, with rugged bluffs and hidden coves. Sand Point, at the western tip, marks the boundary between the Severn Estuary and the Bristol Channel, and St Thomas's Head at the eastern end is a former MOD weapons testing centre. The walk also takes in a house of prayer for the soul of Thomas à Becket, stone walls built by Napoleonic POWs, and boats moored on the mud in a tidal river.

In the summer months, the buses between Weston-super-Mare and Sand Bay are open-topped. They run along the coast road and are worth the fare just for the fun of the journey, even without the glorious walk to follow. The buses turn round at the junction of Beach Road and Sand Road where there's also a car park (BS22 9UE).

Walk towards the sea to turn right along Beach Road. After 250m, turn into Sand Farm Lane and head up past the twin towers of the farm buildings. A gate opens onto a footpath beside a high wooden fence which leads on through a patchwork of small fields with the next gate or footpath sign always in view. Cross a track and step over a stile designed to stop vehicles to continue between hedges to a surfaced road.

Turn left, aiming for Woodspring Priory, easily identifiable by its churchtower. Built in 1210 as a house of perpetual prayer for the soul of Thomas à Becket, the murdered Archbishop of Canterbury, it is

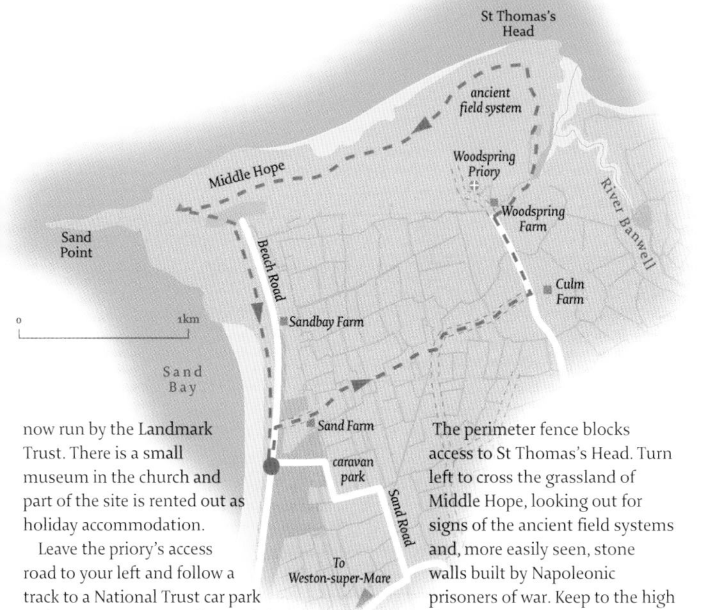

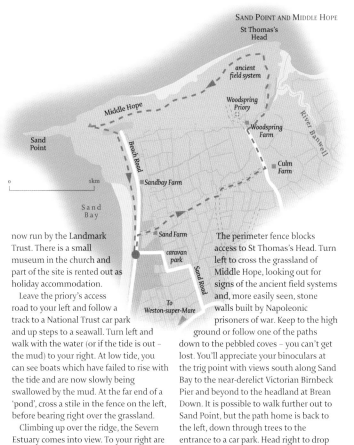

now run by the Landmark Trust. There is a small museum in the church and part of the site is rented out as holiday accommodation.

Leave the priory's access road to your left and follow a track to a National Trust car park and up steps to a seawall. Turn left and walk with the water (or if the tide is out – the mud) to your right. At low tide, you can see boats which have failed to rise with the tide and are now slowly being swallowed by the mud. At the far end of a 'pond', cross a stile in the fence on the left, before bearing right over the grassland.

Climbing up over the ridge, the Severn Estuary comes into view. To your right are the two Severn Bridges; ahead are the Black Mountains of Wales, with Newport just across the water and Cardiff slightly to the west. Behind fencing to your right is an old MOD weapons testing site and World War II air gunnery and bombing range.

The perimeter fence blocks access to St Thomas's Head. Turn left to cross the grassland of Middle Hope, looking out for signs of the ancient field systems and, more easily seen, stone walls built by Napoleonic prisoners of war. Keep to the high ground or follow one of the paths down to the pebbled coves – you can't get lost. You'll appreciate your binoculars at the trig point with views south along Sand Bay to the near-derelict Victorian Birnbeck Pier and beyond to the headland at Brean Down. It is possible to walk further out to Sand Point, but the path home is back to the left, down through trees to the entrance to a car park. Head right to drop down onto the foreshore, then left for the walk back to the start.

You'll know when to leave the beach when you see the elevated conservatory of the Sand Bay tearooms, conveniently placed a few yards from your destination.

◂ Middle Hope

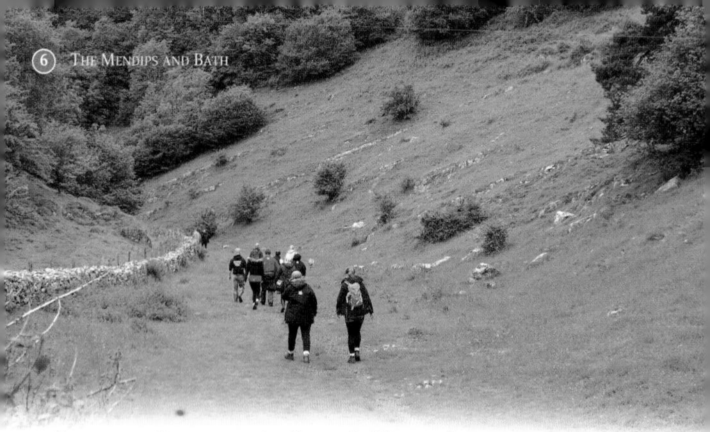

Charterhouse's lead-lined Velvet Bottom

Distance **8km** Time **2 hours 30**
Terrain **paths, fields and tracks**
Map **OS Explorer 141** Access **no public transport to the start**

It's hard to imagine what Charterhouse must have looked like when lead mining was at its peak. These days the shallow valley is a pastoral delight, but in the 19th century this was every inch an industrial landscape. The valley was so polluted that rioting broke out among the people who lived downstream. Today it is rolling grassland, alive with birdsong and even heron on the ponds. Look closer and the ground is littered with relics of the old days. Without the industrial archaeology, this would be simply another enjoyable walk. With it, it's fascinating.

The locals call it 'gruffy' ground, where the old mine workings have left a hummocky, uneven surface covered by hollows and bumps. From the crossroads by the Charterhouse Outdoor Activity Centre, turn up the road with a postbox in the wall to find the car park. Here the ground is at its gruffiest (BS40 7XR).

Return to the vehicle entrance gate and join a path heading left. Walking down to a road, the rocks to your right are the remains of Roman mine workings. Britain was a major source of lead for the Roman Empire and, at Charterhouse, they also anticipated finding silver. They built a fort nearby to protect the site and a small amphitheatre which is passed near the end of the walk. As it turned out the silver content was low, but there was plenty of easily accessible lead.

Turn right when you reach the road, then go left after 50m into Velvet Bottom Nature Reserve. As you follow a wide path down the valley, evidence of more recent mining operations is all around. First, with round 'buddles' where the ore was washed, then a dried-up reservoir, before the path runs alongside extensive dumps of black glass-like lead slag. Further down are several

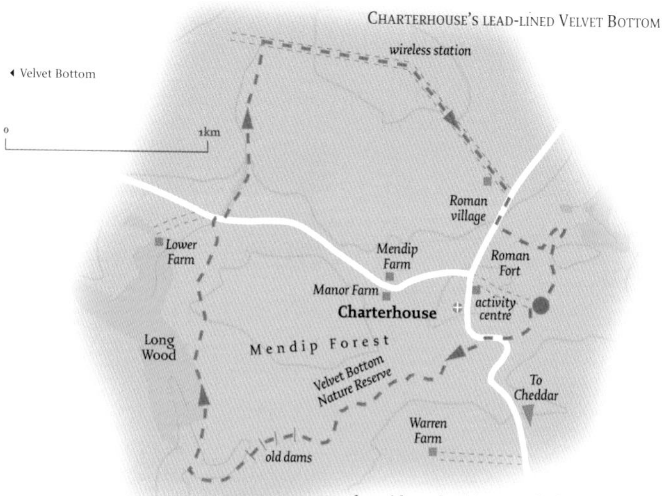

dams made to hold back the contaminated water. Before they were built, pollution downriver was so bad that locals tried to destroy the mine workings by smashing the equipment. The path leads past the dams, each more derelict than the last, until you find yourself walking beside a stone wall.

About 30m short of an information board where valleys converge, take a path up the bank on the right. Cross a stile, then continue up a field to a gate on the skyline. After keeping close to the woods on the left to reach the next gate, bear right across a field to the far side, then follow a wall to reach the corner. A flagstone acts as a stile and a marker points diagonally across a field towards trees visible over the brow.

Cross a stile and follow the path over a stream to a road. Rejoin the path on the other side and, with a wooded gully to your left, climb up the hillside. On reaching open ground, continue on the same bearing before turning right on a path between rough hedgerows. Follow this to the base of the wireless masts, enjoying good views north to the Bristol Channel and southwest to Bridgwater Bay.

Turn right onto the surfaced road where the remains of the Roman amphitheatre can be seen clearly in the field. Some 400m further downhill, the remains of a Roman mining village are less visible in the field below a bungalow. Turn right on the road for 150m before taking a footpath heading left. You re-enter the lead-workings on a wide slag path and, although the route ends over to the right, it's worth making a quick detour left to some impressively large blocks of slag and the remains of the stone-built flues. From here, pick up a path back to the car park.

Cheddar Gorge

Distance **5.5km** Time **2 hours 30**
Terrain **paths, in places very steep and rocky; slippery when wet**
Map **OS Explorer 141** Access **buses from Weston-super-Mare and Wells**

Cheddar Gorge is one of the great natural wonders of the British landscape. Created before the last ice age by floodwaters carving through the limestone, the water now flows underground through vast caverns which are still being explored. The famous caves provide ideal conditions to store the even more famous cheese while it matures. Cheddar is an extraordinary place and attracts hundreds of thousands of visitors every year. While you may never find true solitude on this walk, it's quite possible to escape the crowds to enjoy nature at its most awe-inspiring.

There's plenty of parking at the gorge's commercial centre near the village, but to enjoy a quieter start leave your car at the side of the B3135 as you approach the gorge from the east, just by the 'Welcome to Cheddar Gorge' sign.

Face the sign to take a rocky path on the left, heading uphill by the end of a stone wall. The path climbs steeply through trees to a gate and onto more open ground. Continue to a marker post and, ignoring the sign to Draycott, take the path which goes right. It leads through a tall gate and up beside a fence until you can see the top of cliffs to your right. Now just follow the path, keeping a safe distance from the edge, as it leads along the southern side of the gorge. Don't take risks!

Crossing the highest point, with the Pinnacles to your right, the reservoir and

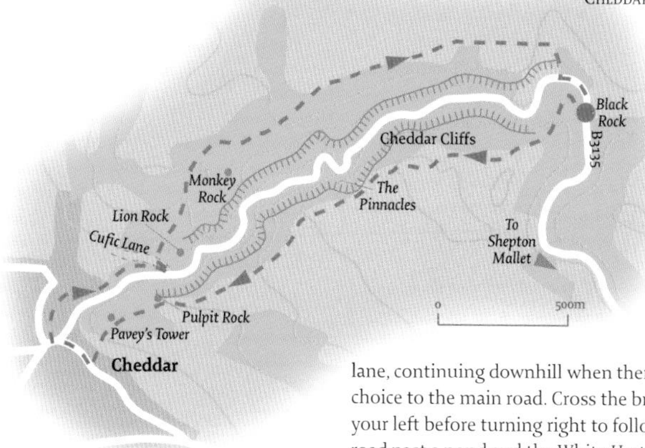

Cheddar village appear ahead. From here it's a steady walk downhill, passing the appropriately named Pulpit Rock, to the viewing platform called Pavey's Tower. The present metal structure dates from 1936, replacing the earlier one built by eccentric entrepreneur Rowland Pavey 30 years earlier. Pavey installed 'Jacob's Ladder', a flight of 274 steps leading from the gorge to his 'Joyland Pleasure Garden', with his 'Mystic Tower' as its centrepiece. At one point, he attempted to fly across the gorge from the tower using home-made wings, but landed in the gorse bushes on the clifftop.

The path heads left about 30m before the Tower, but you might be tempted to climb to the viewing platform before moving on. It provides a fine view up the gorge and across the Levels to the Quantock and Blackdown Hills. Ignore the sign to Jacob's Ladder and return to the path (which will now be on your right). Walk down through the trees and go right when you reach a lane, continuing downhill when there's a choice to the main road. Cross the bridge to your left before turning right to follow the road past a pond and the White Hart pub and onto a surfaced footpath beyond.

After climbing some steps and passing the point where the underground river surfaces, the path heads back to the road beside a row of white cottages. As you turn left into Cufic Lane – a track leading immediately behind the cottages – don't miss Lion Rock which sits on the hillside above the houses. Some 70m up the lane, look for a National Trust sign and steps to a gate on the right. The next leg is a long strenuous climb up the hillside. It is hard work but full of interest with caves in the woods and feral goats to keep you company.

The worst is over when you pass through a gate near the top. Bear right towards a stone wall and, walking more gently uphill at this point, follow the path along the north side of the gorge. Take the flight of wooden steps that descends from the high ground back to the valley floor, where a right turn brings you back to the road. Cross with care before turning left to follow the verge to the start.

◂ Cheddar Gorge

Priddy and the drove roads

Distance **7km** Time **2 hours 30**
Terrain **paths, lanes and quiet roads**
Map **OS Explorer 141** Access **buses between Keynsham and Wells via Priddy on Tuesdays only**

Standing on Priddy Green, it's strange to think that beneath you is a network of underground caves so extensive it has yet to be fully explored. Swildon's Hole is very popular and there are often several groups of cavers down there at the same time. While they explore the damp, dark caverns below, for the rest of us the ancient byways at ground level hold as many delights and fewer risks. This circumnavigation of Priddy village follows old drove roads along which farmers once took their livestock to market.

Priddy Green, where there is a small parking area, is notable for the little thatched stack of sheep hurdles sitting by the roadside (BA5 3BB). The hurdles were used to build pens for the annual sheep fair which dated from the 14th century. A fire destroyed the stack in 2013, but the village quickly built the replica which stands on the green today.

From the stack, keep the green to your right to pass the bus shelter and old telephone box – which now serves as a library. Bear right into Pelting Drove, signed to Deerleap and Wookey Hole. Soon after passing the last house on the right, take a footpath which sets off over a stile on the left-hand side. Part of the West Mendip Way, it leads along the edge of fields, with a right and left turn, until you can turn left on a broad stony track. This is Dursdon Drove and you can follow it, in the footsteps of generations of farmers and livestock, for the next 800m.

In the days before road transport and

◂ Sheep hurdle stack, Priddy Green

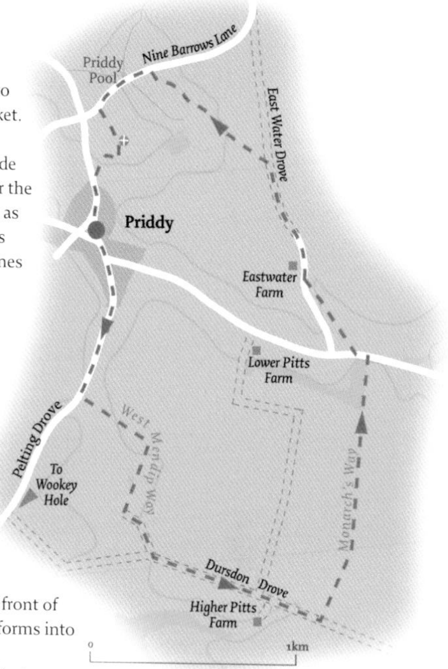

railways, drove roads were used to herd cattle, sheep or pigs to market. They were enclosed by walls or hedges to prevent escape, but wide enough to allow for grazing. Over the years they were either taken over as part of the road network or left as rights of way to become green lanes and pathways.

After passing the entrance to Higher Pitts Farm, walk for a further 200m to turn left onto Monarch's Way. Be careful not to miss the turning; the marker and path are hard to spot. Now follow the left edge of several fields to reach a road. Go left for 40m and cross a stile on the other side. Bear left and walk towards the double gables of Eastwater Farm. Turn right on East Water Lane, in front of the farm, and follow it as it transforms into the unsurfaced East Water Drove.

As you walk, the hill to your right is peppered with Bronze Age sites, including the Priddy Nine Barrows and the Ashen Hill Barrows. Although the drove will lead you to the public road at Nine Barrows Lane and back to the village, it can be soft underfoot and, unless it is the driest of weather, not a very pleasant experience. Instead, look for a footpath which leads off into the pastoral scene on your left. Facing the churchtower, bear right and walk down across the fields, through a scruffy hedgeline and into the corner by a clump of trees. The path goes past a pumping station, then along the edge of a field into Nine Barrows Lane.

Turn left and walk down past Priddy Pool on the right, and then turn left to cross a field into the churchyard. Continue out the other side, between school buildings, and turn right. Follow the road round to the left and walk down the hill back to the village green.

A walk into Wells

Distance 4km **Time** 1 hour 30
Terrain paths, pavements and fields
Map OS Explorer 141 **Access** no public transport to the start but this walk can easily be joined in Wells, which is served by buses from Shepton Mallet and Bath

What Wells lacks in size, it certainly makes up for in medieval architecture. At its heart is the spectacular Gothic cathedral, almost 1000 years old, complete with 300 original statues on the west front. Next door are the moated Bishop's Palace and Europe's oldest residential street. This isn't the longest walk in this book, but with history around every corner it might well take you the longest time.

There is space to park in a lay-by beside the B3139, by the 'Welcome to the City of Wells' sign (BA5 3NT). Across the road a stone stile marks the entrance to woods where a path leads directly up steps to climb the hillside. Cross a stile and bear left to a path – the East Mendip Way – which leads out onto the open grassland of Tor Hill.

Keep the trees close to your left to pass through a gate onto a path down the hillside to Torhill Lane. Turn left and then go right on the public road to walk into town, with the cathedral over to your left, until you then turn left at the Fountain Inn.

As you go along St Andrews Street, you are walking towards Chain Gate, a 15th-century 'bridge' which links the cathedral's Chapter House with the College Hall. Just before it, turn right into the entrance to Vicars' Close. It is 100 years older than Chain Gate and has been occupied since the day it was built by members of the clergy and choristers.

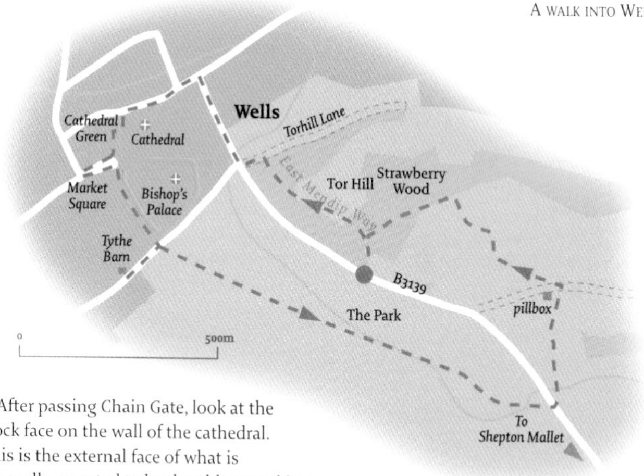

After passing Chain Gate, look at the clock face on the wall of the cathedral. This is the external face of what is generally accepted to be the oldest working clock in the world, dating from medieval times. The interior face includes jousting knights and a drummer who strikes the quarter hour with his heels. It is just one reason among many to visit the cathedral itself if you have time.

To continue the walk, turn left to pass the magnificent west front, complete with 500 statues of religious icons, from Christ and the angels to kings, saints and clerics. Some have been replaced with modern replicas, but 300 of the figures are medieval originals. With the cathedral green to your right, follow the paved path through an arch into Market Square, then turn left, through another arch to the Bishop's Palace. Turn right to keep the moat by your left hand until you reach the turreted corner.

The path back to the start begins straight ahead, but first you might want to turn right for 200m to the 15th-century Tythe Barn, used to store grain which tenants were obliged to supply the church. Head back to the corner of the moat and, with the cathedral behind you, go through the two gates, then keep left along the surfaced path, which leads along the edge of three fields to drop down to join a road.

Cross over, and go through a gate on the other side. Bear left up the hillside, keeping to the right of the wartime pillbox at the top. Cross a track to a stone stile and set out across a field, heading for the far right-hand corner. Walk between hedges, bending right, then left, until you can cross a stile into the woods. Turn left and follow the path along the edge of the woodland. It bends left and right to join the East Mendip Way, close to the grassland at the top of Tor Hill. Head left for 30m, then take the path on the right which, if you retrace your steps down the hillside, will lead you back to the start.

◂ Vicars' Close

Nunney Castle

Distance **5km** Time **2 hours**
Terrain **fields and paths**
Map **OS Explorer 142** Access **buses from Shepton Mallet and Frome**

Nunney Castle is certainly spectacular but, as a fortification, it proved well below the standard required. In 1373, Sir John de la Mare, a veteran of the French Wars, built himself a château in the French style, after receiving permission from the king to construct a 'fortified tower'. It was an impressive house but proved a feeble castle. When besieged in the English Civil War, the occupants quickly surrendered after Roundhead cannons inflicted damage on the north wall. It's been a ruin ever since but a wonderful one and a great end to this walk.

Just above the castle, on Castle Hill, there is a free car park with plenty of space (BA11 4NL). From the entrance, walk a short distance downhill, looking for a gate onto a footpath on the left-hand side.

The path sets off beside a BMX track and out along the edge of a field to a gate. Bear right to a brook where a bridge to the left of a ford helps you across. Turn left to walk beside the water where the riverbank has been sculpted in places for the annual Nunney International Horse Trials. Turn left when the path meets a track to cross a bridge, and then right to continue following the brook downstream.

Eventually the path veers away from the water's edge and climbs to reach a track. Go right and follow the track round a sharp right turn until it ends at the entrance to a field. Now head left, through a kissing gate, and walk along the field edge. Although there's not much to see these days, the land to your right was once the site of a Roman villa, dating from around 300AD.

In the next field, keep to the left edge

◂ Nunney Castle

to find a gate in the hedge. Once through, head for the far right-hand corner, continuing into the next field to walk downhill with a hedge by your left hand. At the next hedgeline, step into the field ahead of you and bear right to walk directly across to a kissing gate on the skyline.

Keep to the left-hand edge of a long field, until you can take a gate between two field gates. Now keep the hedge to your right. After crossing a track to farm buildings, go through a gate onto an enclosed path. Follow it until you can turn sharp left along a wide track and then, after 70m, turn right through a kissing gate.

Now follow the path all the way downhill onto a concrete track and then the public road. Turn left at the junction and then right to walk into the village. After passing the old market cross and the church, look for a path on the right-hand side which leads to a footbridge over to the castle gate.

It's a terrific castle, four storeys high with a round tower at each corner and a wide moat. Nunney's defences went untested for almost 300 years until the Civil War. The castle came under attack when Parliament's forces laid siege to the Royalist garrison in 1645. The defenders quickly realised the walls could not withstand cannon fire and surrendered after two days. The castle was razed to prevent further military use and, although the walls were left standing, the north wall finally collapsed in 1910.

When ready, head back through the gate and walk up the street to Castle Hill, where the car park is up to the right.

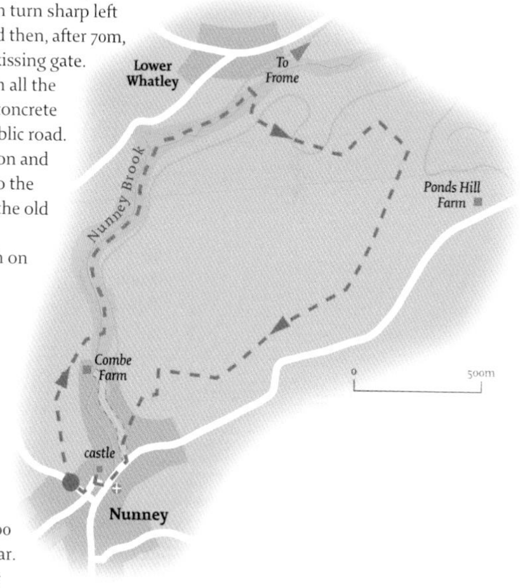

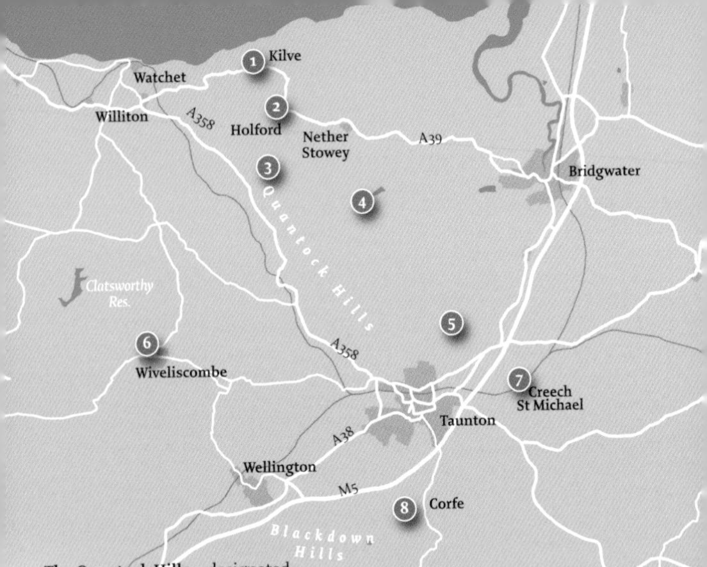

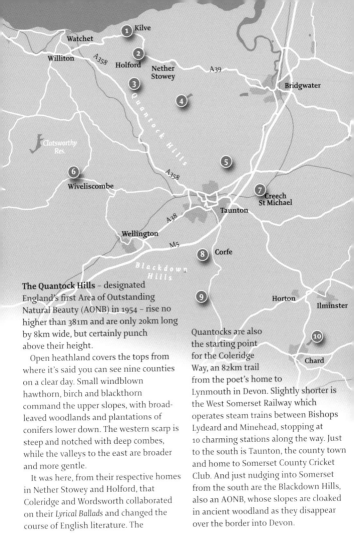

The Quantock Hills – designated England's first Area of Outstanding Natural Beauty (AONB) in 1954 – rise no higher than 381m and are only 20km long by 8km wide, but certainly punch above their height.

Open heathland covers the tops from where it's said you can see nine counties on a clear day. Small windblown hawthorn, birch and blackthorn command the upper slopes, with broad-leaved woodlands and plantations of conifers lower down. The western scarp is steep and notched with deep combes, while the valleys to the east are broader and more gentle.

It was here, from their respective homes in Nether Stowey and Holford, that Coleridge and Wordsworth collaborated on their *Lyrical Ballads* and changed the course of English literature. The Quantocks are also the starting point for the Coleridge Way, an 82km trail from the poet's home to Lynmouth in Devon. Slightly shorter is the West Somerset Railway which operates steam trains between Bishops Lydeard and Minehead, stopping at 10 charming stations along the way. Just to the south is Taunton, the county town and home to Somerset County Cricket Club. And just nudging into Somerset from the south are the Blackdown Hills, also an AONB, whose slopes are cloaked in ancient woodland as they disappear over the border into Devon.

Around the Quantocks

Kilve's Jurassic Coast

Distance **5km** Time **1 hour 30**
Terrain **paths, tracks** Map **OS Explorer 140**
Access **no public transport to the start**

Kilve lies where the Quantock Hills meet the sea. In olden days, the little cove called Kilve Pill was used by smugglers who stored their illicit spirits in a disused chantry close to the beach. That worked well until, in fear of being discovered, one of the smugglers set fire to a brandy barrel to destroy the evidence and blew up the chantry in the process. The shell of the building remains and now shelters a splendid tearoom conveniently near the end of this circuit.

From Kilve village, turn off the A39 into Sea Lane and drive as far as you can to a car park at the end of the road (TA5 1EG).

The square brick construction is a 'retort', a remnant of Kilve's narrow escape from becoming a centre of shale oil production. There were grand plans for developing the area for shale oil in the early 20th century, even a proposal to build a railway to Bridgwater, but they came to nothing. The stone building just beyond the retort sits at the head of Kilve Pill, the creek which, as well as being a smugglers' landing point, was used to bring ashore coal to fuel local limekilns.

Leave the retort to your right and head down to the shoreline, a mecca for fossil hunters who you may see combing the limestone ledges, shale and pebbles. The rock which forms Dorset's famous Jurassic Coast – Lower Jurassic Blue Lias – is also found along this stretch of Somerset shoreline, making it rich in the fossilised remains of creatures which existed millions of years ago. From close up if the tide is out, or from on high as you walk along the cliffs, the foreshore is an extraordinary sight, with curved

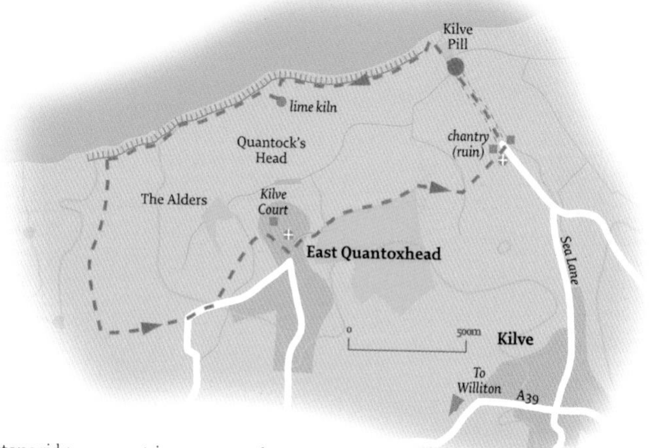

stone ridges, geometric patterns and cobblestone rocks. Overlooked by layered and colourful cliffs, the shore here would certainly have fascinated Coleridge and Wordsworth who walked here in 1797 when they were staying at nearby Alfoxton House.

After searching for fossils, head along the grass above the foreshore and pass through a gate. The path is clear as it follows the cliff line to Quantock's Head, the high cliff directly ahead. Look out for the derelict limekiln a few metres inshore and enjoy the views over to Kilve Court – now an outdoor learning centre. You should also be able to see the Hinkley Point nuclear power station over your shoulder, some 7km to the east.

This is a great spot for blackberry picking (in season) as you make your way along the coast path, turning inland when you see a waymarker to East Quantoxhead. With the hedge on your left, walk up the side of three fields and then turn left onto a farm track leading to a road. Continue ahead for 150m before taking the path on your left directly over a field in the direction of a church and Kilve Court.

Unless you want to visit the church, turn right in front of the gate to walk through the church car park, then right again round the top of the duck pond. With the pond now on your left, take the track beside the pretty thatched cottage and follow it to the fork. Head right to cross fields to reach the road beside the remains of the chantry.

Now propped up by steelwork, these are the remains of a short-lived 14th-century ecclesiastical site, later inadvertently blown up by the smugglers. Call in at the sheltered walled garden behind the chantry for a cuppa before heading left down the lane to return to the start.

◂ The beach at Kilve

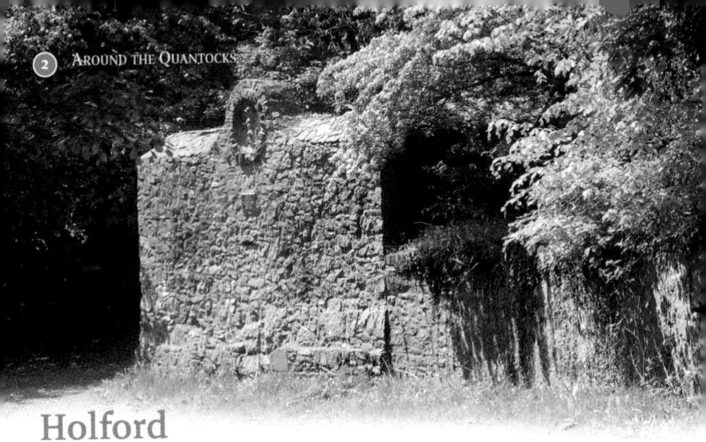

Holford

Distance **5.5km** Time **2 hours** Terrain **tracks and paths, with one stream crossing** Map **OS Explorer 140** Access **buses from Minehead and Bridgwater stop at the Plough Inn, 500m from the start**

Holford is a little village on the edge of the Quantocks which has been touched by greatness. It was here that William Wordsworth and Samuel Taylor Coleridge composed much of their *Lyrical Ballads*, the collection which marked the beginning of the English Romantic movement. Holford Glen meanwhile doubled as Sherwood Forest in Kevin Costner's *Robin Hood: Prince of Thieves* and featured in the music video for the soundtrack song by Canadian rocker Bryan Adams. They were all inspired by the countryside around Holford and it's a fair bet that you will be too.

Don't be fooled by the name when you look for the car park beside Holford's Bowling Green (TA5 1RZ). It's a rough triangle of grass on which, it's claimed, exiled French mill workers played boules when they settled in the area in the 16th century.

From the car park, cross the grass to walk up a road with the green to your left. Soon you come to the Dog Pound, a square roofless stone enclosure topped with the Albyn family crest. Believed to be over 300 years old, the pound was built after a huntsman was killed by his own foxhounds, with stray dogs getting the blame. The story goes that meat for the pack was stored in the branches of trees, a practice which, not surprisingly, attracted strays. The huntsman, who looked after the Alfoxton pack, went to check on his hounds while not wearing his normal hunting clothing and was attacked and killed by his own dogs. Everyone blamed the strays for unsettling the pack so the pound was built to house stray dogs. Slits were built into the walls so people could see inside.

Continuing along the track, Holford Glen

◂ Holford Dog Pound

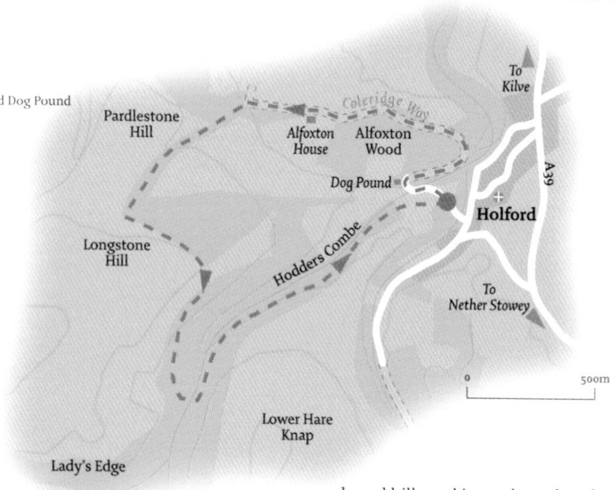

is down to the right behind the deer-proof fence. Just across the stream is the old silk mill where the video for the hit song *(Everything I Do) I Do It For You* was filmed. It sold a remarkable 15 million copies worldwide and still holds the record for the longest unbroken run (16 weeks) at the top of the Official Singles Chart.

The road starts to rise and passes through an avenue of ornamental trees as it makes its way up behind Alfoxton House which looks rather dilapidated these days, having fallen into disrepair since it closed as a hotel. But this once grand house was home to the poet William Wordsworth and his sister Dorothy for a short time during the early years of their friendship with Coleridge. They spent many hours walking the woods and hills and it was here that the two poets composed much of the content of *Lyrical Ballads*, published in 1798 and still regarded as perhaps the most important single collection of English poetry ever published.

Follow the road uphill until it bends sharply right. At this point, go through the gate on the left and head up through trees to the common. Paths head off in five directions; take the second on the left to bear round the shoulder of the hill. A superb view over to the Bristol Channel opens up before the path heads into woods to descend into Hodders Combe. The ground falls steeply to the left, although the hillside is hidden by oak and holly trees for much of the way. At the very bottom, make your way across a stream. From here, with the water to your left, follow the path all the way downstream to return to the Bowling Green.

Triscombe and Wills Neck

Distance **8km** Time **2 hours 30**
Terrain **fields, paths and tracks, including one very steep ascent (a gentler alternative route is provided)**
Map **OS Explorer 140**
Access **buses from Minehead**

It's said that if you sit on the Triscombe Stone, your wish will be granted. If that's true then many dreams will have been fulfilled thanks to this ancient marker stone high in the Quantock Hills. Close by is Wills Neck, at 386m the highest point in the Quantocks, gained by a steep climb from the village below. It's a great place to soak up the view and consider what you might ask of the Triscombe Stone on the way home.

At the top of the steep hill out of Crowcombe the road to Nether Stowey crosses a cattle grid before emerging onto open ground. A parking place soon appears to the left of the road (TA4 4AB).

Walk back along the road, ignoring the wide path heading left in the trees, to cross back over the cattle grid. Turn left through a wooden gate and head out onto the pasture. A clear path across the grass soon becomes apparent, bearing right towards a cairn on the hill. Halfway to the cairn, turn left down to a gate in a wall, and then turn right to descend to the bottom of Little Quantock Combe.

Before reaching a farmyard, take a path up the bank to your left, and follow it as it winds alongside the fences and hedges below Great Hill. After passing through Ladybird Wood, there is a good view of Wills Neck ahead before the path begins to descend to join a track. (This is the point to turn left if you wish to avoid the very steep climb up the face of Wills Neck. Walk up the combe to reach a car park by the Triscombe Stone. From there, turn right at

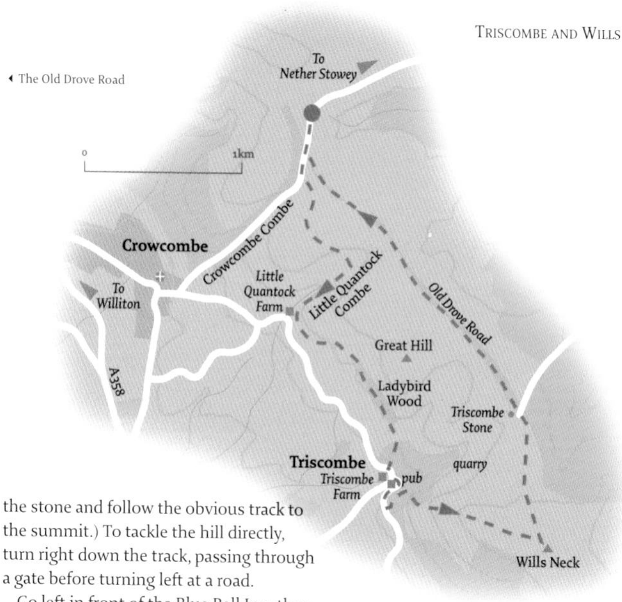

the stone and follow the obvious track to the summit.) To tackle the hill directly, turn right down the track, passing through a gate before turning left at a road.

Go left in front of the Blue Ball Inn, then take the road on the right to walk behind the pub, signposted to Bagborough. After 300m, take the path on the left which heads back towards the village just above the road. Follow the path until a gate on the right opens onto a very steep slope, with a faint path more or less discernible climbing up into the undergrowth. Engage a low gear and set off up the hillside.

As the crow flies, it is roughly 400m until the ground feels like it begins to level off a bit, but over that distance you will have climbed more than 70m. The going is hard but the views from the top – not to mention regular stops to catch your breath on the way up – make it worth the effort: the Bristol Channel and Wales to the north; Glastonbury and the Levels to the east, and the Brendon Hills with Exmoor beyond to the south and west.

Suitably rested, with your back to the trig point face the way you came up the hill. Now bear right on a wide path which goes down the hill to a car park. On the left is the Triscombe Stone which has been here since the Bronze Age. *Tris* is a Celtic word for 'meeting' and the stone is believed to mark the crossing of two very ancient Quantock hill routes.

Continue through the car park along the Old Drove Road, once an important trade route now lined with a stunning avenue of beech trees which provide a guard of honour to lead back to the start.

Aisholt

Distance 9km Time 3 hours
Terrain footpaths (one shared with a stream in wet weather), fields, and public roads; a couple of short steep climbs
Map OS Explorer 140 Access daily bus service between Bishops Lydeard and Bridgwater stops at the western end of Hawkridge Reservoir during Bridgwater College terms

Aisholt is a 'Thankful Village', where every man who left to fight in World War I returned. The village itself is just a small cluster of houses by a 14th-century church, but Coleridge liked the place so much he wanted to live there – until his wife put her foot down. Another poet, Sir Henry Newbolt, lived there after his wife inherited a property in what he described as 'that beloved valley'.

The walk begins from the car park on the south side of Hawkridge Reservoir (TA5 1BD). With the water to your right, set off along the pavement for 250m.

Take the track on the left which climbs into woods on the other side of the road. It leads to a restored limekiln which, in its heyday, would have produced up to eight tons of lime a day to improve the productivity of local fields. It fell into disrepair in the 1930s, but was restored just before the millennium.

Return to the road and turn left. Go right at the junction to walk between the reservoir and a settling pond, a valuable habitat for toads, then turn left onto a bridleway through woodland which is maintained as a nature reserve by the Somerset Wildlife Trust. The path crosses a ford before emerging onto a lane beside a thatched cottage, where Sir Henry Newbolt lived after the Great War.

Head right to walk uphill to steps leading to the church on your left. Inside

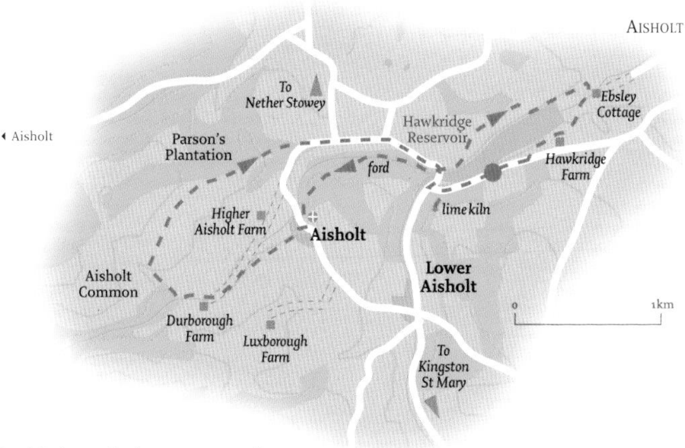

is Aisholt's Roll of Honour, proudly listing the eight men from the parish who fought and survived the 1914-1918 conflict. With the steps to the church on your left, go through a gate on your right. Keep to the left of the field to climb another flight of steps, turning right at the top. Follow the bottom of a field to a track in the corner which leads down, over a small ford, to a road.

Turn left to Durborough Farm. With the farm buildings to your left, head up a track which you may have to share with a stream! When the track opens onto some scrubby woodland, ignore the well-used path that climbs uphill, taking instead the less obvious route immediately to your right, beside the fence.

After 200m the path emerges onto more open ground and your route lies up the steep slope to your right. The ground soon levels out and the path leads straight ahead onto open grassland. Maintain your height as you walk across the common to join a track. Continue and go through a gate to follow the old cobbled surface downhill to a public road. At the junction, turn downhill (right) along a stretch of road which is altogether busier.

At the bottom, opposite the bridleway you took earlier, take the path on your left. It leads through trees and up the left-hand side of fields, offering a good view over the reservoir to your right. Keep the trees to your left until you can cross a double stile in a hedge, then go right to follow the field edge to a stile in the corner. A path now leads through trees to join the drive to a cottage.

Cross a little bridge, and turn right on a path which leads into a field below the dam. Head towards the left-hand side of the dam, over a stile, to cross the road. Initially with a hedge to your right, follow a private road down past the fishing clubhouse, then look for a stile in the hedge to your left soon afterwards. Bear right across the field and turn right along the road back to the car park.

West Monkton

Distance **5km** Time **1 hour 30**
Terrain **paths, pasture and a quiet road to finish; several stiles** Map **OS Explorer 140**
Access **buses between Bridgwater and Taunton stop at Monkton Elm, 800m from the start**

Considering it lies close to the M5 motorway and Taunton, West Monkton is a surprisingly sleepy and tranquil village. It can trace its history back to 682AD when it belonged to the Abbot of Glastonbury, and the church at its centre dates from the 13th century. This short walk starts from the village and explores the quiet fields and combes that surround it.

There is space for several vehicles to park at the side of the road on Church Hill, at the top of Doster's Lane (TA2 8NP). Go downhill and then turn left onto the drive to St Augustine's Church.

Old as the church may be, it's thought that the big yew tree among the headstones is even older, possibly having grown on this spot for 1500 years. Look out too for the 18th-century village stocks, once used for the public punishment of miscreants, now protected from the elements by a wooden canopy. Even rarer, under the same roof, is a whipping post, complete with a set of manacles.

Take the path which sets off uphill from the front door of the church, heading up behind a house. Turn right at the top and walk past cottages to reach a road. Cross over and, after passing through a metal gate, continue up a path to another road. Turn right for 150m and then cross a stile into a field on your left. Now keep to the right-hand side, crossing two further stiles to walk down the hillside.

On nearing the bottom of the valley, bear left through a farm gate and across a footbridge over a stream. Follow the right field margin up the slope to go through a cluster of trees beside an old quarry. In the

◂ Stocks in West Monkton Churchyard

next field, ignore the first gate on the right but go through the second which opens onto a path leading down through scruffy trees to cross yet another stile.

Heading down towards the cottages at Coombe Bottom, bear left to walk with a stream at your right-hand side. After passing through a gate into a field, bear left to go uphill, aiming for the right-hand side of the woodland on the crest. At the top, ignore the gate to your left, but look for one to your right which opens to a path through the trees. Follow the path as it bends left to take you downhill to a track.

Turn right to go through a gate, then right again to walk up a slope with a cottage over to your left. The next gate opens onto a field where you keep the hedge by your right hand for about 200m, before striking out left to cross the field in the direction of a communications mast on the far side. There are great views of the surrounding countryside from here – on a clear day you can see Glastonbury Tor and the Wellington and Burton Pynsent Monuments.

Go through a gate near the foot of the mast to cross the road and walk up the access track to Woodball Cottage. Immediately before the house, a path heads right to lead you gently downhill, before going left round the back of the property. Follow this path down through the holly and rhododendron bushes, back out into a field and into trees once again. Just as it emerges onto a road, you pass the old West Monkton Quarry, the source of the Morte Slate widely used for building walls until the quarry closed over a century ago. Turn right on the road and follow it down the hill and back to the start.

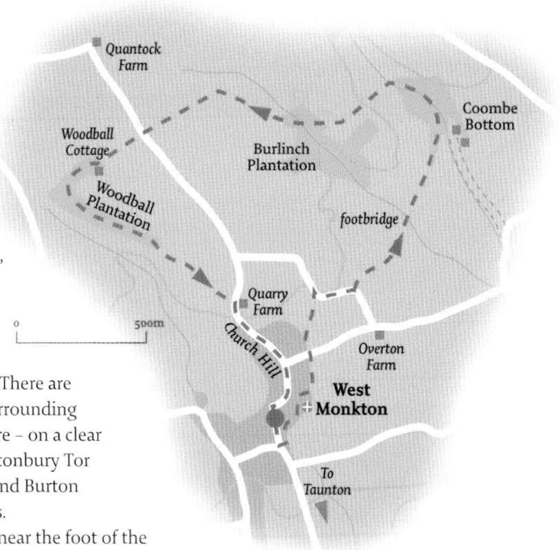

Wiveliscombe

Distance 7.5km **Time** 2 hours 30
Terrain paths, bridleways and pavements
Map OS Explorer OL9 **Access** buses from Dulverton and Taunton

The medieval market town of Wiveliscombe – known as Wivey – makes a lovely starting point for this jaunt into Somerset farmland. Many of the town's older buildings have survived along with a former brewery near the town centre. There is much of interest in both the town itself and the farmland that surrounds it, and the walk is particularly invigorating in the spring when the fields are full of wildflowers and the air alive with birdsong and the bleating of lambs.

There is a free car park in Wivey's North Street, just a short distance from the town centre (TA4 2LJ). Once parked, head left to the town square and then bear left to enter Silver Street, which leads (naturally) to Golden Hill. With old houses lining the route, walk up to a T-junction and turn into Stile Road on the left.

After a few steps, look for the narrow entrance to a footpath on the right, hiding between a house and a wall. There is a sign but it's tucked neatly out of sight inside the entrance. Follow the path to a road and cross with care before continuing up the path on the other side. Go left when you cross a stile, then bear right after the next stile, aiming to the left of the old stone ruin. Walk up the side of two fields where another stile leads onto a path. When you get the chance, look back over Wivey. Unusually for an English town, it's not dominated by a church spire; instead the tallest building is the

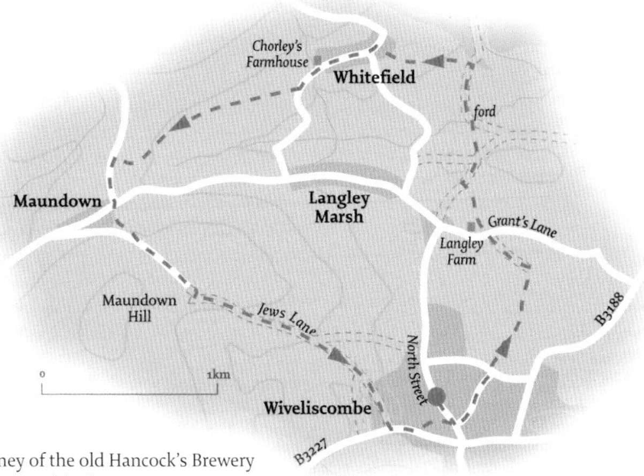

chimney of the old Hancock's Brewery which closed in the 1960s.

Cross a road when you come to it and head up the track opposite. After passing a sheep shed, leave the farm gate to your left and follow a track on the right. Keep the hedge by your left hand and follow the path as it leads uphill to a T-junction at the crest. Take the footpath which continues straight on down a steep field where a stile is waiting at the lowest point. Now follow a sunken footpath up the slope until it bends to the right. Climb left up a flight of steps, then set off across fields, passing through gates as you make your way to Whitefield.

Walk behind houses to a lane and go left. Keep right at the fork and head on down past Chorley's Farmhouse and the next cottage on the right. Now take a footpath on the right. This leads across the fields, maintaining the same direction and going through gates until you find yourself walking through a tunnel formed by overgrown hedges. Emerging into a field, the right of way follows the field margins to your right down to a road. Go left on the road and straight across the next road to head up the metalled driveway to a path which begins between two upright posts designed to deter horses.

Go left when you reach a road and follow it to the top of the hill. Head left and then right for the long walk down to the town. This is Jews Lane, an ancient sunken bridlepath which leads all the way down to Wivey, ignoring a path up to the left, and another which forks up to the right to continue all the way down the hill and into the town. Turn left at the bottom along West Street. You may feel the need to nip into a shop and reward yourself with an ice cream, before turning left again back to the start.

◂ Wiveliscombe Court House

Creech St Michael

Distance **8km** Time **2 hours 30**
Terrain **towpaths, riverbanks and mostly quiet roads** Map **OS Explorer 128**
Access **buses from Wells and Taunton stop in St Michael Road, close to the start**

For the River Tone, the opening of the Bridgwater and Taunton Canal must have been like the arrival of a motorway in modern times. The Tone was navigable but the canal was faster. Soon the railways had made both river and canal redundant as a means of commercial transport, but for walkers they are easily linked and make for a wonderful outing.

There's a perfectly placed car park at the end of Vicarage Lane, right by the towpath of the canal (TA3 5PR). Set off along the towpath, with the canal on your left and follow it in peace and tranquility for the next 2km.

The canal was opened in 1827 as part of a grand plan to link the English and Bristol Channels. The Bridgwater and Taunton Canal effectively bypassed a long bend in the River Tone, but by 1907 traffic had all but ceased and the canal was closed. The cause of its demise lies close by and you may see and hear trains passing along the railway line across the field. Keep close to the canal, first on the towpath and later when it becomes a track, until you reach the red-brick span of Charlton Bridge, probably the best preserved of the original canal crossings.

Turn right to cross the railway line, then left. Walk straight ahead from the

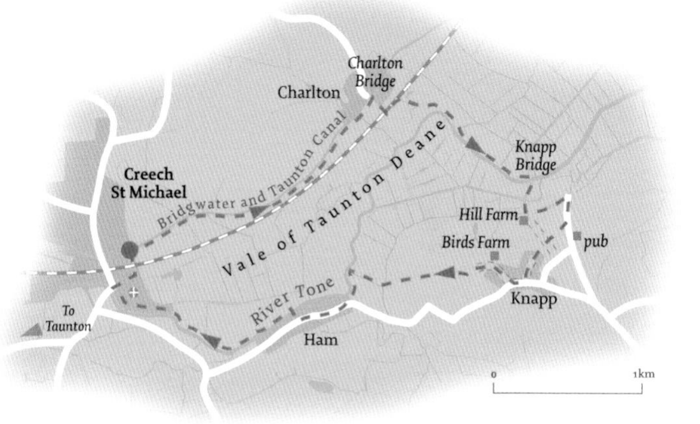

bottom of the ramp along a farm track until you have passed through a gate. Now turn right along a path which winds round beside a hedge to join the River Tone. Keep to the path along the river's north bank, with the water to your right, for around 700m to Knapp Bridge.

Cross the river and head along the track for 200m, where a left turn will take you along the edge of a field to a stile. Turn right along a quiet road which leads to the Rising Sun public house if you need refreshment. Our path goes right shortly before the pub comes into view. Look for a stile, slightly hidden in the hedge on the right.

Once over it, and the rickety one soon after, bear left to the corner of the field. Cross the drive to Hill Farm and then head across two fields to join a road. Go left and climb up a gentle hill, keeping right at the fork. Turn right at the junction to walk along Knapp Road for 20m. Bear right into Higher Knapp Lane and follow it until you can turn left opposite Birds Farm. After another right turn the road surface ends with stables on your right. Go through the entrance, then keep close to the left-hand edge of the orchard to join a path leading through woodland and down field margins to the river.

Turn left, passing a suspension bridge, and right at a road. Walk into the hamlet at Ham, keeping an eye out for a footbridge to cross the river on your right. Now bear left, staying close to the riverbank as you head back towards Creech St Michael. The name is thought to derive from the Saxon *crug*, meaning 'hill', although as the landscape is so flat, some people believe it is simply a derivation of 'creek'. On reaching a pillbox, leave the river and bear left along Bulls Street, turning right into Vicarage Lane soon after passing the church. Turn left at the T-junction to return to the car park.

Blagdon Hill

Distance **8km** Time **3 hours**
Terrain **paths (some of them muddy), field edges and a minor road; wellies recommended after wet weather**
Map **OS Explorer 128** Access **early morning and late afternoon buses between Taunton and Buckland St Mary stop in Blagdon Hill**

Blagdon Hill is not a hill at all. Straddling the old highway between Taunton and Devon, it is a typical turnpike village which is surrounded by attractive farmland and overlooked by the ancient woodlands of Adcombe and Prior's Park. This walk into the Blackdown Hills is a floral delight in the spring, but perhaps at its best amid the golden browns of autumn.

Parking is not easy in Blagdon Hill, but there are some spaces just off the main road at the north end of the village (TA3 7SD). This is actually the village green, although it must be one of the smallest in the country. It's a slightly awkward walk for 400m along the main street, where you need to look carefully to spot a footpath sign, pointing left to a metalled access road between stone walls.

The footpath begins by electricity transformer poles and runs along the left edge of two fields. Cross a footbridge and climb some steps before setting off round the left side of a field to a gate onto a lane. Walk down the lane towards the church spire in Pitminster – the original settlement in the area – until you are nearing farm buildings.

With a gate into the churchyard on your left, head right and follow the path to a footbridge through a hedge, bearing slightly right over the next field. Continue in the same direction over the next field to pass a tin shed. After crossing a stile, walk

◂ Prior's Park, Blagdon Hill

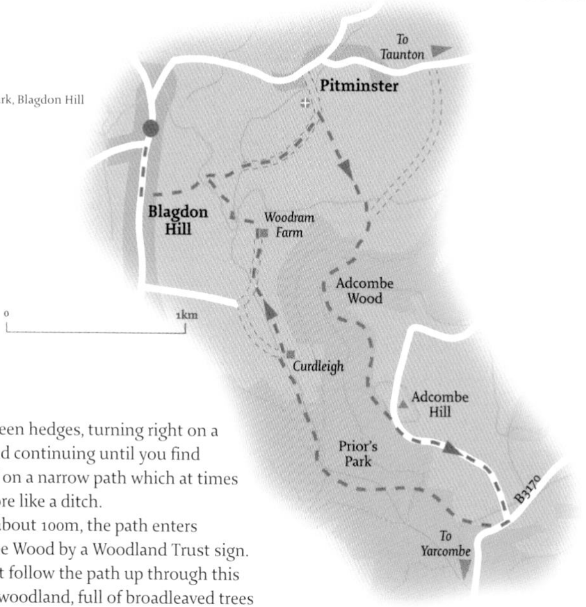

up between hedges, turning right on a track, and continuing until you find yourself on a narrow path which at times feels more like a ditch.

After about 100m, the path enters Adcombe Wood by a Woodland Trust sign. Now just follow the path up through this ancient woodland, full of broadleaved trees - oak, ash, and hazel - which are typical of the Blackdown Hills. Following the contour, close to the top of the woods with fields to your left, look out for bluebell or wild garlic if you are visiting in the spring.

Where the path joins a lane, head right and walk downhill, then up again to a road. Go right for about 20m before heading down the track on the right into Prior's Park. Leave the track where it swings left and continue downhill on a narrow path which will probably be muddy as it nears the bottom of the valley to pass a water sump - part of the efforts to prevent flooding downstream on the Somerset Levels.

When the path reaches a track, turn left and follow it down through woods beside the stream. Cross a bridge when you come to a farm access track and walk along the opposite bank between houses. Continue along the edge of a field to a gate in the far corner and join the track up to Woodram Farm.

Leave the old farmhouse to your right and soon after take the track heading left across a field and then over a stream. Bear right, then keep to the left edge of the field. Ignore the farm gate and look for the stile in the hedge to your left soon after. From the stile, you can retrace your steps back into Blagdon Hill.

Otterhead Lakes

Distance **2.5km** Time **1 hour**
Terrain **paths and tracks**
Map **OS Explorer 128**
Access **no public transport to the start**

In its heyday, Otterhead must have been a magical place. The pleasure grounds at the heart of the estate boasted seven ornamental lakes, two walled gardens and several acres of landscaped terraces and driveways. Together they made Otterhead House a haven of tranquillity for the privileged few who could enjoy it. The house was demolished in 1952, the gardens have disappeared and only two of the lakes have survived, but what remains amounts to a lost Victorian landscape. It's still a special place and, what's more, nowadays we can all enjoy it.

The easiest way to find Otterhead is to follow signs to Otterford Church from the B3170. The church is roughly 300m along the road from the Otterhead Lakes car park (TA3 7EE).

Set off downhill past the information board with the former lodge house to your right. Soon you join the old main drive, passing the crumbling ruins of walled gardens, with the House Lake (or Top Lake) down to your right.

Otterhead House was on the far side of the water and 100 years ago the view would have been of lawns, ornamental gardens and a tennis court. Between 1817 and 1864, the orchards and woodlands in the valley were transformed to complement the mock-tudor mansion. By the early 20th century, the house was tenanted and upkeep of the grounds no longer a priority. The last gardener left in the 1930s and slowly the place has been returning to wilderness. Even so, the floral displays remain impressive, starting with snowdrops which thrive in the woodland, followed by narcissi and bluebells in spring, then rhododendrons in July.

Don't cross the bridge, but take the path which heads left just before it to walk

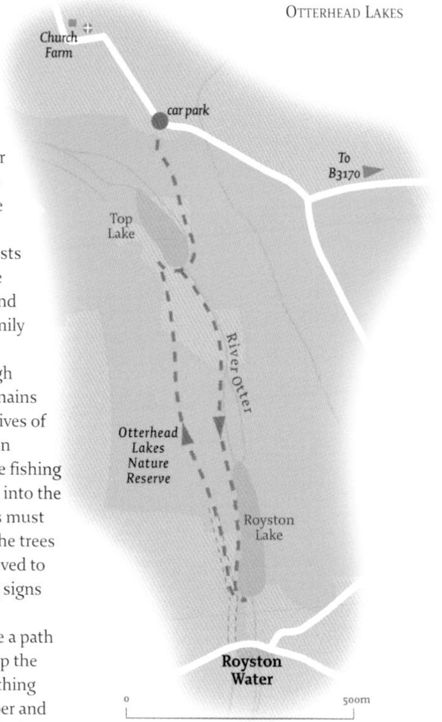

◂ Otterhead

beside the river, soon crossing over a footbridge. The River Otter, in its Somerset infancy here, reaches the sea some 30km downstream. Uniquely for an English river, it hosts a population of beavers. They were hunted to extinction in England and Wales in the 12th century but a family was spotted on the Otter in 2014.

Following the path down through the woodland, look out for the remains of sluices to your left, all that survives of the original ornamental lakes. Soon Royston Lake comes into view. The fishing is let to an angling club and a gate into the private fishing area means walkers must bear right to join a track. Among the trees on the banks are field maple, believed to be over 250 years old and showing signs of historic coppicing.

Bear left and, when you can, take a path down to the weir for a view back up the lake. It is a good place for birdwatching and you may spot kingfisher, dipper and wagtail among others. Royston Lake has been a source of water supply for Taunton since the 1930s. The house was demolished because of concerns that its continued use might contaminate the water supply.

From the weir, retrace your steps to rejoin the old lane and bear right to walk with the lake now over to your right. Follow the path up through a plantation of conifers until you see the gable of the old coach house, now a Forest School. Bear right and walk up past the school to explore the area where the house, garden and tennis court used to sit.

Steps lead down towards the lake beside the entrance to a small waterwheel chamber where water was once pumped up to the house. It takes a leap of imagination to picture a fine Victorian mansion on this spot, but there is plenty to interest the curious before heading back past the school, turning left to cross the bridge for the walk back up the drive to the start.

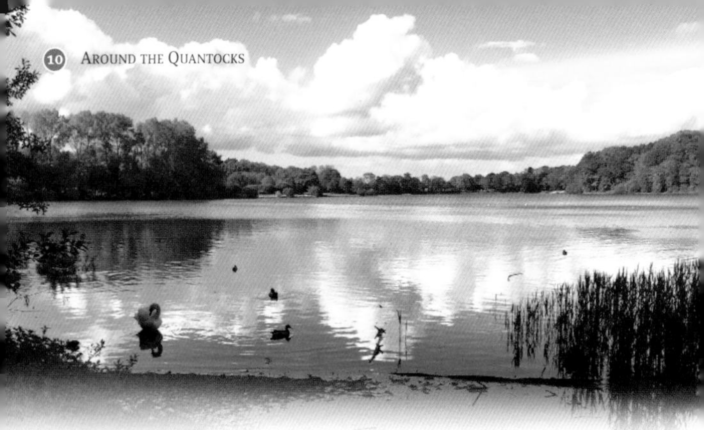

Chard and Chaffcombe

Distance 7km **Time** 2 hours 30
Terrain path, fields and quiet roads
Maps OS Explorer 116 and 128
Access buses from Axminster and Taunton stop in Chard, a 15-minute walk from the start. Dogs are not allowed on a section of the reservoir path

The Chard Canal was never a success. Completed in 1842, it required four aqueducts, three tunnels, four inclined planes and a reservoir for the barges to travel just 22km. It lasted for only a quarter of a century before being made redundant by the new-fangled railway. For many years the reservoir, which fed the canal, was used for shooting and fishing before being taken over by the local authority. Now a nature reserve, the water levels are managed to encourage nesting birds in the spring and to help prevent flooding in the winter. All year round it is a wonderful place for birdwatchers and walkers alike.

The Chard Reservoir car park is at the far end of Oaklands Avenue, just off the A30 Crewkerne Road (TA20 1HU). With your back to the vehicle entrance, take the pathway that heads over to the left to cross a road into the reservoir's parkland.

Keep to the right-hand side to pass through a line of trees, then bear left over a footbridge onto a path leading down towards the water. Turn right onto a broad surfaced path which meanders through the trees with the water over to your left. You will pass a gate, beyond which dogs are not allowed. At the top of the reservoir, where the wide path bears left, take the narrower path which heads uphill to the right.

At the top, step left to join the public road and then turn right to follow it up through the cluster of houses at Chaffcombe Gate Farm. Here the road bends right and then starts to climb up the side of Sprays Hill. Where it levels out at the top, a stile is hidden up by your right shoulder, giving access to a field. Skirt the

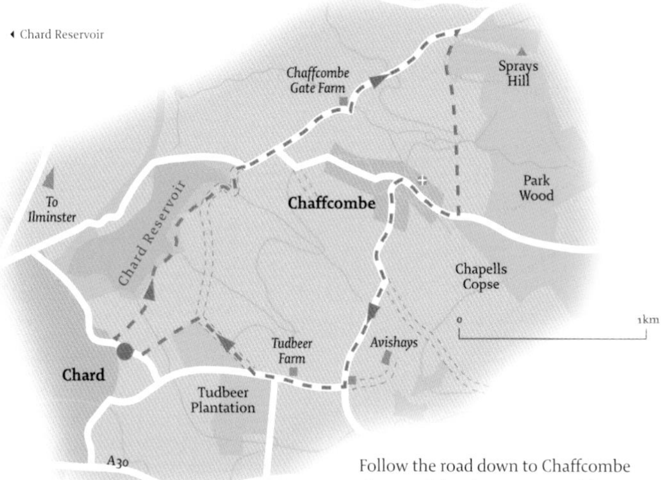

woodland to your left with wide views out to your right over Chard and to Ilminster behind you.

The path ends with gorse to the right and a stile into a field. Head out across the grass, keeping just to the right of the trees in the middle. You may have to pass through a gate in an electric fence on the way, as you walk down to the bottom of the slope. Look for a stile hidden in a fence below an impressive oak tree.

Head straight across the woodland, over a footbridge, then maintain the same direction across a field. Keep to the right margin of the next field until you step through an unusual gate to turn right on the public road.

Follow the road down to Chaffcombe and on reaching the war memorial, turn left and continue up the hill, bearing right at the 'No Through Road' sign. There's a good view of the house at Avishays over to your left. Behind the 18th-century mansion is the Monmouth Tower, a folly housing a hand-wound clock, which originally came from Highclere Castle in Hampshire.

On reaching Avishays Lodge, turn right and follow the road for 500m to join a track bearing right. When the woodland ends on your left, cross a stile and follow a narrow path down to the bottom, then continue on the same line across the next two fields. Turn right when you reach a surfaced lane and, although you will soon be able to see the start point through the trees on your left, you must walk 100m further to reach the path which will lead you there.

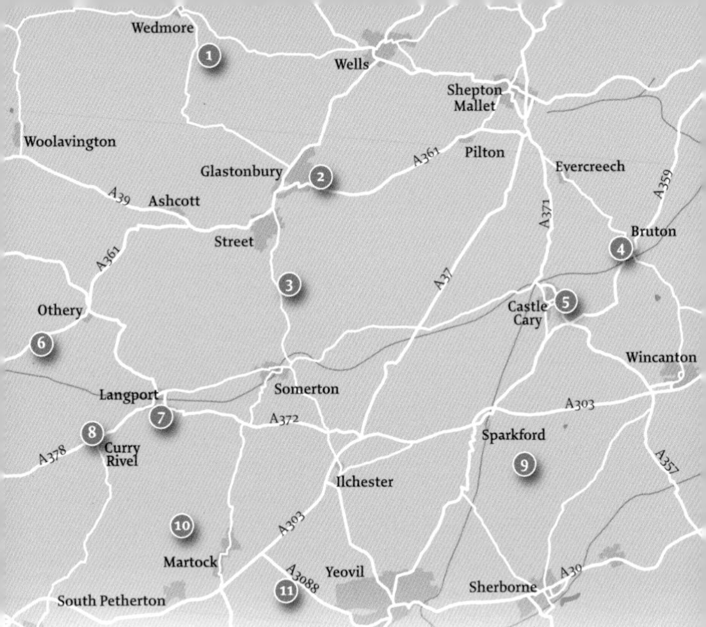

If any part of Somerset can be accused of grabbing the headlines, then it's the Levels and Moors. Glastonbury Festival attracts the world's best live bands and performers in the summer and prolonged spells of wet weather bring fears of flooding in the winter. Thousands of years ago, this low-lying flat ground between the Mendip and Quantock Hills was covered by seawater, but today it's a wide, flat and unique landscape of wetlands, crisscrossed by droves (tracks) and rhynes (ditches) and relying on artificial drainage and pumping stations to control the water level. Sudden hillocks and bumps – dry islands when this was marshland – rise up to interrupt the view. Most famous is that Somerset icon, Glastonbury Tor, which can be seen from almost anywhere. At its foot is Glastonbury itself, once the site of the South West's biggest abbey and now a mixing bowl of beliefs and faiths – over 70 at the last count.

While legend, supported by only the sketchiest of evidence, suggests that King Arthur's Camelot was in this part of Somerset, beyond doubt is the part the area played in helping King Alfred defeat the Danes. From his hideout in the marshes, he rose to establish the kingdom of Wessex and lay the foundations for the unification of England. Rich in wildlife and marinaded in history, the Levels and Moors are a special place indeed.

Burrow Mump ▸

Around the Levels and Moors

Westhay Moor

Distance **6.5km** Time **2 hours**
Terrain **paths, tracks and very quiet roads**
Map **OS Explorer 141** Access **no public transport to the start**

If you want to experience the Somerset Levels, then Westhay Moor Nature Reserve is the place to do it. In prehistoric times, this was part of a vast freshwater wetland; neither land nor sea but somewhere in between. Over the ages it has been drained and reclaimed providing rich farmland and a valuable source of peat. Today the old peat workings have been transformed into a wildlife habitat of international importance. Somerset Wildlife Trust's reserve allows us to see the landscape as it might have looked 1000 years ago; a patchwork of wetlands, lakes and reedbeds alive with birdsong and wildlife.

There's a free car park on Dagg's Lane Drove, just off the B3151 Westhay to Wedmore road (BA6 9TX). From the car park entrance go right on a path beside a track until you see a bird hide on your left, the first of several on the walk. It is always worth popping in to a hide to see what's around. Look out for reedbed specialists like the Cetti's and reed warblers, and perhaps a bittern – or an otter – if you are lucky.

Take the path to the left of the hide, lined with birch, alder and Scots pines, and follow it between lakes created by historic peat extraction to the London Drove. There's plenty of interest along the way. Look out for the wooden starling sculpture in celebration of the spectacular murmurations – one of the Levels' most iconic wildlife spectacles which can often be seen over the reserve in the winter months.

You might be tempted to visit the tower bird hide 200m off the path to the right. From its raised viewpoint, it is easy to

◂ Heron at Westhay Moor Reserve

imagine what the Levels were like before the Romans first began to drain them. To the hunter-gatherers of prehistoric times, the Levels were a waterlogged but rich environment ripe for exploitation. They moved between islands of dry land on wooden walkways, some timbers of which have survived from around 4000 years ago.

On the left are signs to the 'Mire', a rare patch of lowland acid raised bog. Before the drainage and peat extraction, mire was commonplace in the Levels, but now this is the only surviving example of the habitat in South West England.

You'll know London Drove when you come to it: a wide track which you join at a crossroads. Turn right and follow it for the next 1.5km, over a wide rhyne (pronounced 'reen'), and then turn right onto North Chine Drove, a quiet surfaced public road. After 250m, take the gate on the left and go directly across the field, over a rhyne, and across the next field.

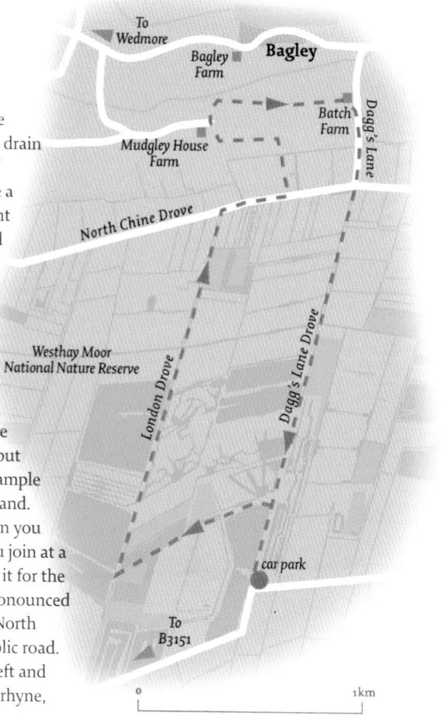

Turn left to walk with a hedge on your right to the corner, then head up to the right on a concrete track beside an orchard. Turn left at the top for a few paces until you can go right, on what looks like the surfaced path to a house. Continue on grass to a path leading through the undergrowth and up the hillside. Where the gradient becomes less steep, cross a stile to your right and step into the field. You can now look down over the Levels and trace the route by which you arrived.

Turn left, keeping below the fenceline to walk along the top of several fields, before a marker post by a gate tells you to bear right in front of Batch Farm. Go through a gate and turn right on Dagg's Lane. After 400m, cross the road and continue on the lane which is now called Dagg's Lane Drove straight back to the start.

Glastonbury Tor

Distance **7.5km** Time **2 hours 30** Terrain **pavements, paths and quiet roads** Map **OS Explorer 141** Access **buses from Bristol, Wells, Yeovil, Bath and Taunton**

Let's face it, you cannot visit this part of Somerset without climbing to the top of what is probably England's most iconic hill. Glastonbury Tor, rising like a beacon from the Levels, is steeped in myth and legend and is a place of pilgrimage for both Christians and pagans alike. You might have to work hard to reach the top, but you'll certainly be awe-struck when you get there.

If arriving by car, head for the Draper Sheepskin factory just off the A361 from Shepton Mallet (BA6 8DB). The company is based close to the Tor and has a small area available for public parking for a nominal fee. Otherwise, from Glastonbury's High Street, put St John's Church on your left and head up to the junction where a right turn, and 700m of pavement, will bring you to the entrance to Draper's factory across the road.

From the car park, turn right to pass Chalice Well and then left into Wellhouse Lane soon after. Take the footpath on the right which leads up the hill past a National Trust sign; it's a steep climb, but on a firm path with steps to help. The Tor has been a place of pilgrimage since Neolithic times and thousands of people make the climb to the top each year, drawn either by its religious significance or just by the outstanding views.

The summit is more than 150m above the surrounding countryside and on a clear day the views in every direction are breathtaking. A topograph just over the summit points out the highlights and

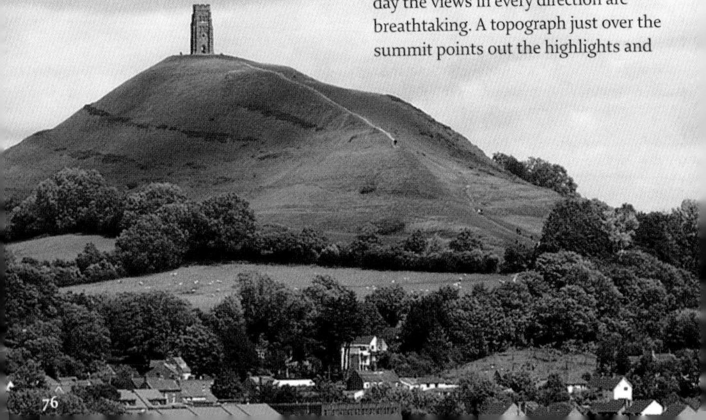

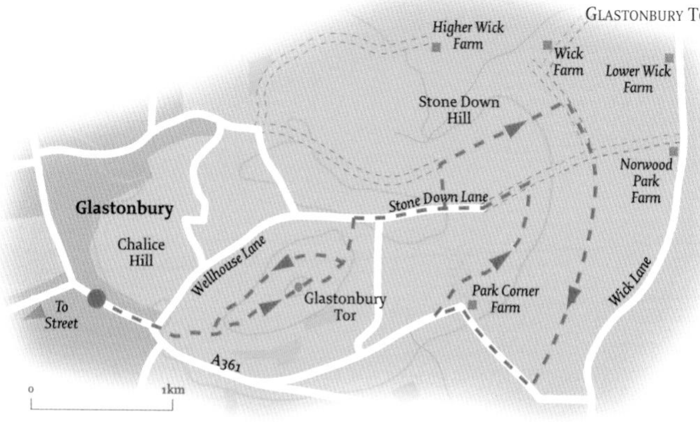

in good visibility you might even be able to make out the main stage at the Glastonbury Festival site some 8km away, on roughly the same bearing as Cranmore Tower. The tower on the tor is all that remains of a 14th-century church which was demolished during the Dissolution of the Monasteries in 1539. At the same time, Thomas Cromwell had the last Abbot of Glastonbury, along with two monks, hanged, drawn and quartered on the tor for treason.

From the summit, with your back to the path by which you arrived, take the steps on the right-hand slope down to the bottom of the hill. Go through a gate where a concrete path leads to a road. Turn right along Stone Down Lane for 100m, continuing ahead when the road bends sharply right. After a further 200m, turn left onto a permissive footpath and then right on reaching a field. Now keep close to the left-hand margin with glimpses of the low-lying orchards, fields and houses at Wick through the hedge.

As you start to walk downhill, look ahead where the old oaks, Gog and Magog, are visible in the hedgeline. Gog is in a pretty bad way, not helped by a fire in 2017, although Magog still shows visible signs of life. Known as 'The Oaks of Avalon', they're believed to be 2500 years old and may once have been part of an avenue which led up the tor.

Once through the gate, a short detour left will take you to the oaks but to continue the walk, turn right. Follow the path behind the caravan site to Stone Down Lane. Cross and continue on a path through several fields. Go right when you reach Gipsy Lane, walking uphill past the Glastonbury Spring Water Company before turning left. After 150m, cross a stile by a National Trust sign and bear right to walk around the bottom of the hill.

Keep the hedge to your right until you reach Stone Down Lane. Turn left and walk along the lane back into town, or head back over or around the tor to retrace your steps.

◂ Glastonbury Tor

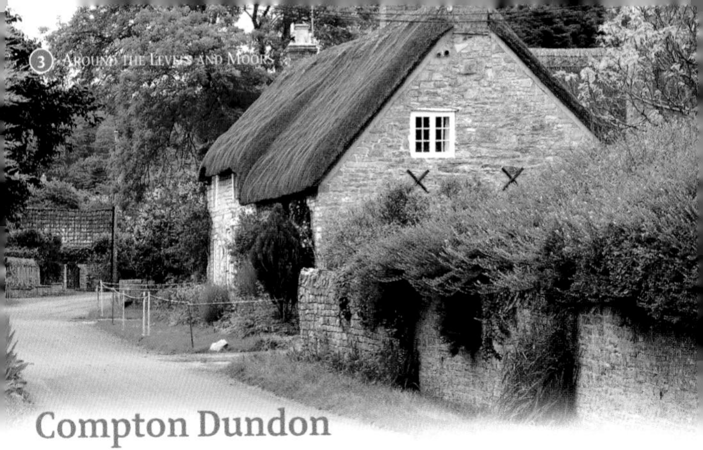

Compton Dundon

Distance **8km** Time **3 hours**
Terrain **hill paths** Map **OS Explorer 141**
Access **buses between Yeovil and Wells stop at Marshall's Elm road junction, close to the start**

The top of Dundon Hill has been transformed since it became a nature reserve some 40 years ago. The fir trees have been cleared, leaving a careful balance of ancient oak woodland, hazel coppicing and restored grass downland. With its long history, peaceful setting and abundance of wildlife, Dundon Hill is a wonderful place for a picnic. The walk also visits a memorial to a naval hero and one of the oldest trees in the country.

The National Trust provides free parking just west of the crossroads at Marshall's Elm (BA16 0TZ), 400m along the road signposted to Bridgwater.

With your back to the youth hostel, cross the road and bear left on a path leading through the woods and back to the junction. Cross the B3151 carefully to pick up the path on the other side as it leads through a gate and onto Collard Hill. As you cross the grass, keep close to the fence on the left. There are superb views over to the right where Dundon and Lollover Hills rise from the Levels.

After passing through the next gate, keep a sharp lookout for one of the country's rarest butterflies, the Large Blue, which was declared extinct in Britain in 1979 but has since been successfully reintroduced on Collard Hill. The best time to see it in flight is in June or early July. Soon the crown of the Hood Monument is visible, towering above trees ahead.

The path leads through a series of gates, across a road, then up Windmill Hill. The monument commemorates Vice Admiral Sir Samuel Hood, who served with distinction in the Napoleonic War (among others) and earned enough respect for this 35m tower to be paid for by public subscription. Originally it looked east, along an avenue of cedars leading to his family home. Today it has a good

◂ Compton Dundon

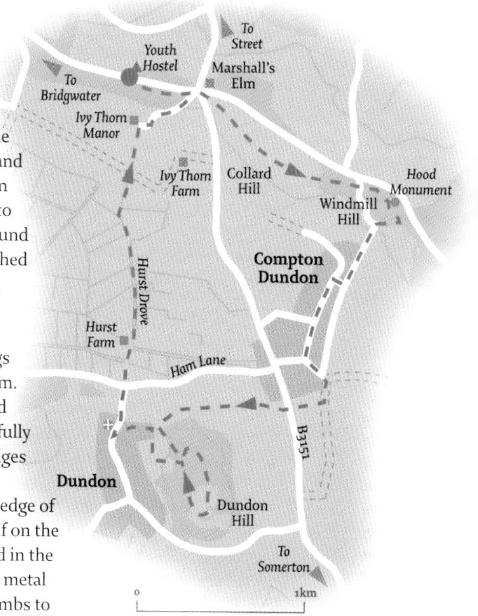

view north to Glastonbury Tor.

The path continues beyond the memorial, before turning right and winding downhill to a road. Turn left and after 400m bear right into Compton Street and follow it round to the left. As you pass the thatched house and shed at Willeys Farm, it's easy to imagine how this street looked a century ago. Go left when Compton Street swings right and follow the lane for 300m. The path then leads across a field on the right. Cross the road carefully and rejoin the path between hedges on the other side.

Follow the footpath along the edge of four fields until you find yourself on the Church Path, with flagstones laid in the 18th century. Turn left, passing a metal gate and follow the track as it climbs to the Dundon Beacon Nature Reserve information board. After exploring the hilltop, return to the board and head back down the track, soon turning left to pass a gate and then turning right down the slope, meandering between anthills.

At the bottom, head left along School Lane and, at the junction, take a short detour to visit the church. It dates from the 14th century but the huge yew tree in the churchyard is thought to be twice as old!

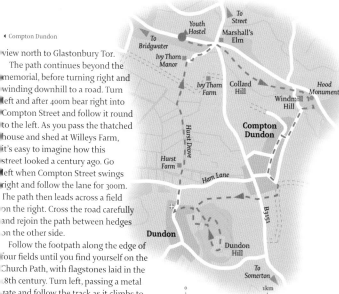

Return to the road and turn left along Peak Lane. Go straight over the crossroads and onto Hurst Drove, leaving the cricket pitch to your left. After 750m, pass an agricultural shed and step left onto a path which continues along the side of fields, crossing a track before joining a surfaced path to the gates of Ivy Thorn Manor. Bear right to follow the road up to the junction at Marshall's Elm.

It was on this slope that the first skirmish of the Civil War took place in August 1642. A contingent of Parliamentarians was ambushed as it came up the hill. Cavalry then chased it back down again. As you approach the road junction, turn left onto a path back to the youth hostel.

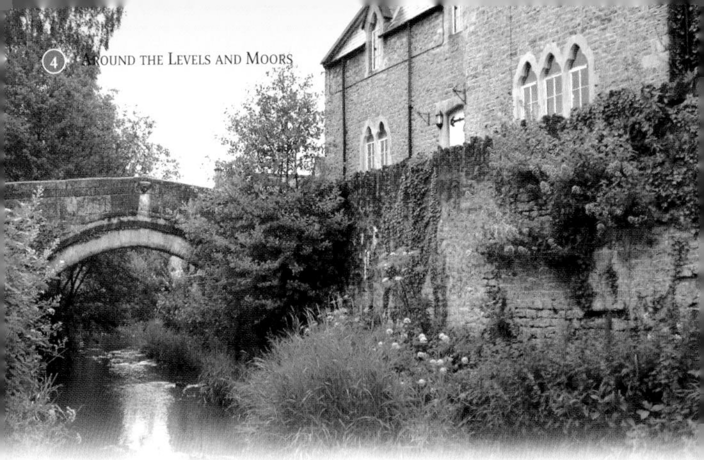

Bruton

Distance 9km Time 3 hours 30
Terrain paths, fields, country roads and plenty of stiles Map OS Explorer 142
Access buses from Wincanton, Street, Yeovil and Shepton Mallet. Bruton Station is a 10-minute walk from the town centre

Bruton has become something of a magnet for the rich and famous in recent years, earning it the accolade of 'Somerset's Notting Hill'. There is a buzz about the place, with three public schools, a packhorse bridge and a famous set of stepping stones over the River Brue – not to mention the internationally famous Hauser & Wirth contemporary art gallery.

There's a small car park in Higher Backway which is signposted from Bruton's High Street (BA10 0DP) or roadside parking away from the town centre. Make for the west end of the High Street by heading away from the library, until past a letterbox set in a wall on the left. Just beyond, turn right into Mill Dam, a narrow lane which leads up through trees to a ford.

At the end of the ford, turn right to the top of the hill, where a footpath – Huish Lane – leads to the left between overgrown hedges. Follow it for almost 1km up the hillside until, soon after a sharp right and left turn, you pass a solitary farm shed on the left.

At the next field gate, turn right and, once past the livestock sheds, turn right again. Walk up a track which is shared by tractors and walkers. Soon it becomes a sunken path, climbing up the hillside, before emerging into daylight again at Creech Hill Farm. Leave the farmyard to the left as you head along the access road, with good views over the surrounding countryside to the right. You should be able to see Alfred's Tower poking its head above the trees to the east.

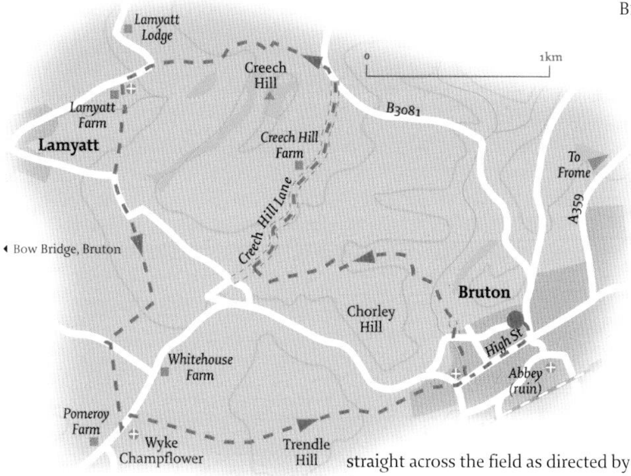

Turn left on reaching the public road, but only for 50m, to a gate on the left. Bear right across the field, straight out past the electricity pole. Once over the brow of Creech Hill – with views now to the west – a gate opens to a track which winds its way down the hillside to join a road. Turn left and walk downhill for 200m towards Lamyatt.

Go left again at the sign for Lamyatt Church to walk through the churchyard and into the right-hand corner of the field beyond. The path drops down to cross a stream, then climbs right to a gate into a field. Ignore what may be a more clearly defined path bearing right, and head for the house behind the hedge at the top of the field in front of you.

At the left end of the hedge, a couple of stiles lead onto a quiet road where you should turn left. When the road bends sharply, cross the stile on your right and go straight across the field as directed by the footpath sign, looking for a stile in the far hedge. In the next field, aim for the right of the house with a white dormer window set into brown roof tiles. Beside it, a stile gives access to the public road.

Go left for 30m to a stile on the right. Now set off across the field, bearing left. Make for the double field gates near the far end of the hedge to your left which open onto a road. Go left for about 70m, then take the stile on the right and head out across the fields, climbing stiles as you come to them. After crossing a concrete farm track, bear left to find a stile hidden in the top corner of the field. Now turn left where a path leads between hedges.

Follow the path all the way down the hill to the bottom of Bruton's High Street, with a good view over to the castle-like dovecote on the other side of town. Time permitting, seek out the old stepping stones and 15th-century Bow Bridge over the River Brue before you leave.

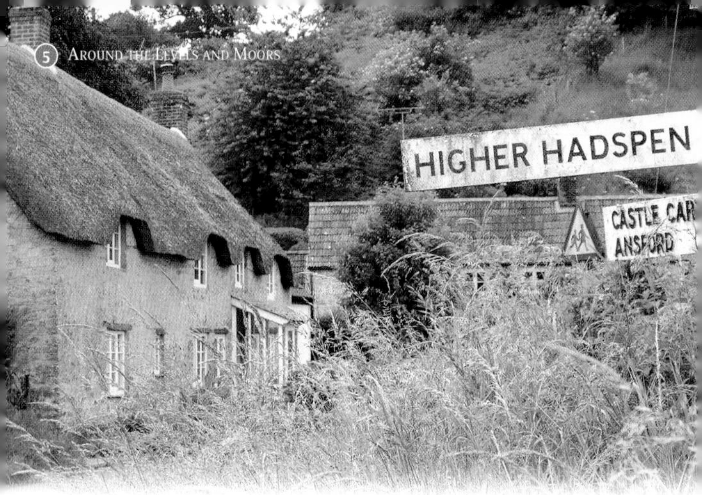

Castle Cary

Distance 5km **Time** 2 hours
Terrain paths, tracks, fields and lanes
Map OS Explorer 142 **Access** buses from Wincanton, Street, Yeovil and Shepton Mallet; the train station is 1.5km north of the town

Castle Cary has long since disappeared, but the town which bears its name is thriving. Independent shops and bustling eateries line the main street, alongside venerable buildings like the Market House, the thatched George Hotel and the 18th-century Roundhouse jail. An important cloth producer over the centuries, Castle Cary is one of the few places in the world where horse hair fabric is produced on a commercial scale, using machinery which dates back to 1870.

Castle Cary proudly boasts that parking is free and provides a generous long-stay car park – in Millbrook Gardens at the lower end of the town (BA7 7EE) – to prove it.

Walk back to the main road and turn left, passing the Horse Pond, a remnant of the castle moat, as you head up Fore Street to the Market House, a 19th-century building housing a very modern community centre within. Turn right into Paddock Drain by the George Hotel, where an interesting information board with details about the town and its history is attached to the wall. Take a footpath which sets off between stone walls and climbs out of the town.

When the path enters a field, keep to the left as you walk up Lodge Hill, with the former site of the castle over to the right. The path bends right as it reaches the top from where you can often see many of the strange hills that rise from the Somerset

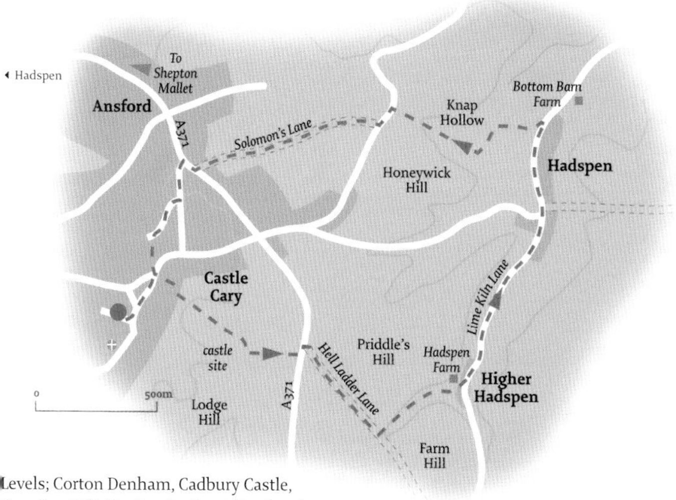

Levels; Corton Denham, Cadbury Castle, Hamdon Hill, Montacute, Brent Knoll and, of course, Glastonbury Tor can all be seen from the summit.

Cross a stile in the left-hand hedge and walk directly across a field, turning left when you reach a road. After 30m, turn right into Hell Ladder Lane and follow the track down to the bottom of a valley. Before the path begins to rise again, go through a gate on the left to walk along the contour until the path drops down into an orchard at Hadspen Farm.

Turn left along Lime Kiln Lane to pass a road junction with the village hall on your right. Around 400m beyond, take a track on the left which doubles back on the road for a few metres before heading along the side of an orchard. The path bears left through trees before turning right to ascend through Knap Hollow, with the ground rising on either side. On reaching a road, turn left for around 70m and then join Solomon's Lane on the right.

Follow the lane for 800m to emerge onto the busy A371. Cross with care: turn right for a few paces and then turn left into Ansford Road. Around 150m down the hill, turn right into Catherine's Close and, soon after the car park, look for a blue sign pointing left to the shopping centre where a path takes you down into the old town.

Go right at the bottom to visit the old lock-up, where vagrants and crooks were held before they faced the judge. To see inside, borrow the keys from the butcher's shop opposite. Walk on downhill to return to the main street and retrace your steps to the start from there.

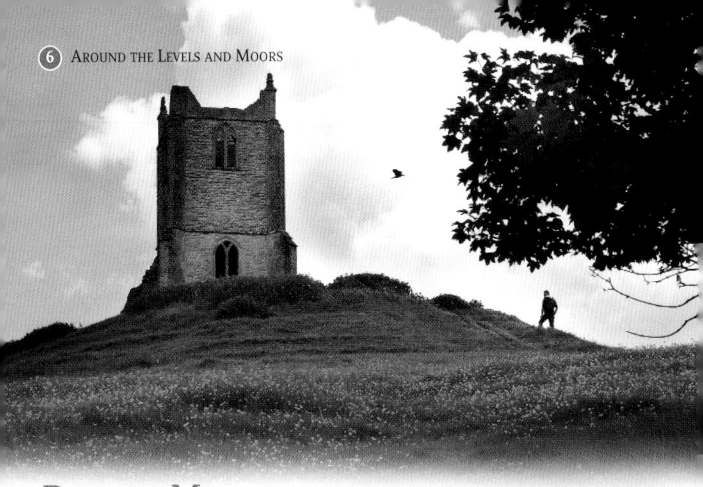

Burrow Mump

Distance **8km** Time **2 hours 30**
Terrain **paths, tracks and a country road**
Map **OS Explorer 140** Access **buses from Taunton and Wells**

The roofless church which stands on Burrow Mump has seen a bit of action over the years. It may not have been built when Alfred the Great came to scan the marshes for Danes and it probably looked a bit different when Royalist troops took refuge here in the 1640s; and then again when the king's army occupied the hill a few decades later. Now it serves as a war memorial to the men and women of Somerset who died in World War II. Burrow Mump marks the start and finish of this otherwise flat circuit along the river and rhynes.

The National Trust provides a free car park beside the A361 at the foot of Burrow Mump (TA7 0RB). Road signs to Burrowbridge will direct you there.

Both 'burrow' and 'mump' mean the same thing (hill) and the walk starts with a climb straight to the top. It is only 24m high, but the views from the summit are hard to beat and, if you can imagine what the area was like in King Alfred's day, you can understand why this was a special place. The Mump dominates the nearby Rivers Parrett, Tone and Cary, which acted as thoroughfares across the marshes before the levels were drained. St Michael's Church on the summit may look like a ruin but, in fact, it was never completed and has always been a roofless shell. The hill was given to the National Trust in 1946 as a memorial to those who died in Word War II.

From the church, the path sets off directly towards the village of Burrowbridge where steps and a gate lead down onto the busy main road. Cross

◂ St Michael's Church, Burrow Mump

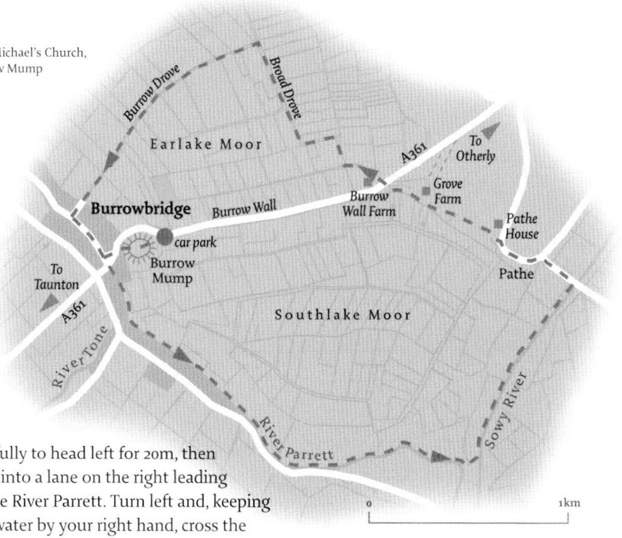

carefully to head left for 20m, then turn into a lane on the right leading to the River Parrett. Turn left and, keeping the water by your right hand, cross the main road again and set off down the track beside the King Alfred pub.

Soon the path passes the confluence with the River Tone; continue to follow the riverbank for the next 2km. When the river bends more sharply to the right, take the footpath signposted left by a gate. A short crossing over grass brings you to a wide rhyne called Sowy River, which you should have at your right hand for the next 1km. On the way, look out for heron fishing for eels and for crane which have been reintroduced to the Levels after an absence of 400 years.

On reaching the road turn left and left again at a T-junction in Pathe. After 250m, with a high brick wall beside you, turn left to pass a wrought-iron gate onto a metalled access track. Take the grassy path which sets off uphill until a marker post directs you down the slope to the left into a field. Follow the right-hand field edge to skirt Grove Farm, then keep to the left-hand field margin to reach the A361.

Cross over the road and set off up the track beside Burrow Wall Farm buildings. The track follows a narrow rhyne, turning right, then left, then right again to run between pollarded willow trees along Broad Drove. Turn left when you can onto Burrow Drove and follow the track back to the riverbank. Another left turn returns you to Burrowbridge where you can retrace your steps over (or round) the Mump to the start.

Langport and Muchelney Abbey

Distance **6km** Time **2 hours**
Terrain **paths, fields and a quiet road**
Map **OS Explorer 129** Access **buses from Yeovil and Taunton**

You can blame Henry VIII for the fact that there's not much left of Muchelney Abbey. But, when he razed the principal buildings in 1538, he left some parts standing, including the Abbot's residence, Priest's House and – uniquely in Britain – a two-storey thatched lavatory. The abbey is a peaceful spot in a picturesque setting and the highlight of this gentle excursion into the Somerset Levels.

If something appears slightly strange about Bow Street, the main thoroughfare in Langport, it's because the houses are leaning gently backwards. It's thought that their fronts benefit from sitting on the foundations of a Roman causeway. The town hall, towards the eastern end of the street, has a distinctive protruding clock, opposite which is the entrance to a free car park (TA10 9PR).

At the far side of the car park, take a path which leads to the riverside walk by the River Parrett and turn right. Until the coming of the railway, the river, now on your left, brought traders here and allowed Langport to thrive as a market town. It was also the scene of an important battle in the Civil War, when the Royalists were outnumbered and outgunned by Cromwell's New Model Army. The defeat all but destroyed Royalist morale in the West Country, with Bridgwater falling soon after.

After almost 400m cross the river on a footbridge, bearing left on the far bank to a road. Turn left to pass an animal feed plant on the right-hand side. Look for the entrance to a path on your left, between

◂ The Priest's House

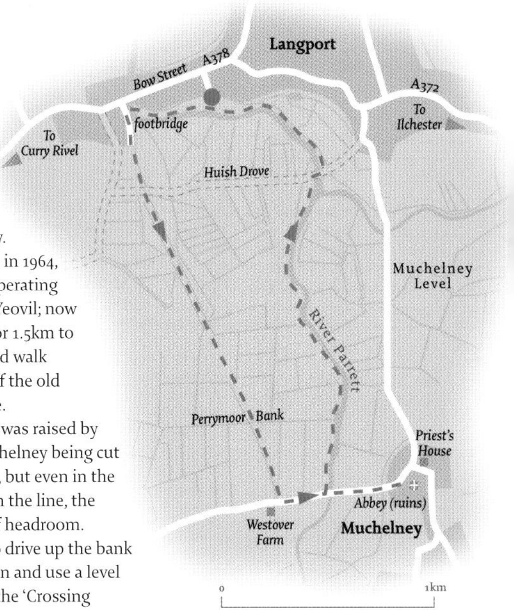

barriers designed to allow only walkers to pass, and follow the path to a track. Go right for a few steps, then turn left onto the bed of a disused railway. Until the Beeching cuts in 1964, this was a branchline operating between Taunton and Yeovil; now it will lead you south for 1.5km to join a road. Turn left and walk between the parapets of the old Westover railway bridge.

In 2014 the road level was raised by a metre to prevent Muchelney being cut off in any future floods, but even in the days when trains ran on the line, the bridge had only 2.1m of headroom. Anything higher had to drive up the bank you've just walked down and use a level crossing controlled by the 'Crossing Keeper' who lived in the cottage.

Follow the road for 500m to Muchelney Abbey, in its time second only in size to Glastonbury. Even though the abbey building itself was destroyed over four centuries ago, the foundations show that this was a substantial ecclesiastical site. Other buildings have survived, including a two-storey thatched lavatory block known as the 'reredorter' or, more appositely, the 'necessarium'. It is the only one of its kind still standing.

The nearby Priest's House, opposite the church porch, was built in the early years of the 14th century. (Separate admission charges apply for both the abbey and the Priest's House.) Muchelney sits on slightly raised ground, and once formed an island in the marshes, a status it reclaims when the Levels flood.

When you are ready to move on, head back along the road to cross the river, then take the path on your right along the embankment, with the water to your right. On reaching the next bridge, cross the river and turn left. Follow the Parrett back to Langport.

Curry Rivel and the monument

Distance 7km Time 2 hours 30
Terrain paths, fields and quiet roads
Map OS Explorer 128 Access buses from Yeovil and Taunton

The Burton Pynsent Monument is an impressive tower erected for an unusual reason: 18th-century cider baron, Sir William Pynsent, was so grateful to the Prime Minister, William Pitt the Elder, that he left him his estate, much to the surprise (and probably annoyance) of Pynsent's family. The two men apparently never met, but Pitt had opposed increasing the taxes on cider and Pynsent never forgot it. In gratitude, Pitt commissioned the tower which still stands on Troy Hill and dominates the surrounding countryside.

Curry Rivel – named after the 13th-century Lord of the Manor, Sir Richard Rivel – is blessed with a stunning Grade I listed church and free parking. Try the car park off Church Street or find a space at the roadside (TA10 0HE).

Walk uphill to pass the church and turn left into Butt Lane. After 150m, take a gate on the left and follow the path across a field, bearing left to enter some trees before reaching a road. Cross over to walk up the lane opposite, ignoring the old iron kissing gate on your left, and pass behind a long shed onto a path leading up the side of a field. Cross a fine stone stile, then continue to walk ahead over two fields before stepping left onto a footpath to a road. Go right along the road where, after 180m, a footpath heads left by the gatepost to Stoneley House.

Keep to the left side of a field to a stile where, soon after, you can turn right to walk up an avenue of trees to the monument. It was designed by the celebrated landscape architect Capability Brown and looks out over the Levels to the north. On a clear day, there's a fine view

◂ The Burton Pynsent Monument

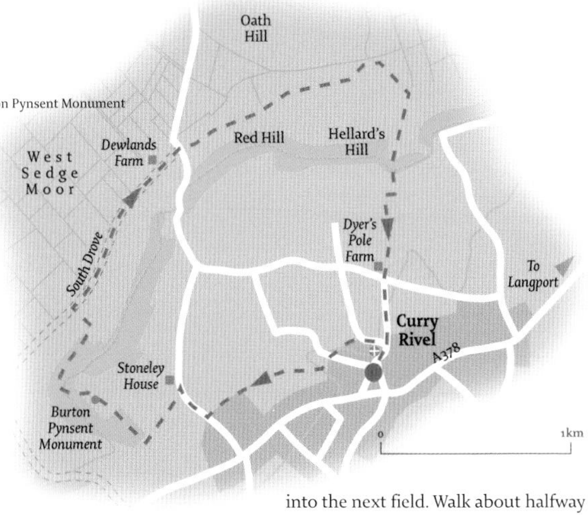

towards the site of the Battle of Sedgemoor, 12km to the northwest, where the Duke of Monmouth's rebel army was finally annihilated in July 1685 in the last battle fought on English soil. Slightly further west, but a mere 5km away, is Athelney which, in ancient times, was a low island in the marshes, notable as Alfred the Great's stronghold in 878AD before he fought back and finally routed the Danes.

With your back to the avenue of trees, continue over the hill to a gate where the path descends the hillside, turning right at the bottom. When the path enters a field, a stile is visible in the hedge on the other side, where you should bear left to join a lane. Turn right to follow the lane to a T-junction at Dewlands Farm.

Go right for a few steps, then left to walk the length of a field and cross a stile into the next field. Walk about halfway along the next field to a stile hidden in a kink in the hedge. Bear gently away from the right-hand hedge, cross into the next field and walk to the far end, keeping to the right-hand side. When you enter the next field, bear left to the corner by a rhyne, cross the next narrow field and then strike out right, heading for the far corner by a cluster of sheds hiding in the trees. Don't cross a stile, but turn right through a gate and walk to the top right-hand corner of the field, where the path leads up into woods by a fence.

At the top, follow the path along the right side of a field before turning right to walk along the back of a house. Turn left just after the driveway and garage to go down the side of two fields, through a farmyard and across a road. The lane ahead leads into Curry Rivel, passing the church on its way back into the village.

Cadbury Castle

Distance **10km** Time **3 hours**
Terrain **quiet roads, fields and paths**
Map **OS Explorer 129** Access **buses to Chapel Cross on the A303, 850m north of the start**

It's said that on dark winter evenings you can hear King Arthur and his knights riding out from Cadbury Castle; Camelot's spectral horsemen and hounds passing on their way down the hillside. In use from the Stone Age through to the Saxons, archaeologists say there was never a 'proper' castle with battlements, turrets or drawbridge on the site, but they have shown that someone built a mighty citadel there after the Romans left. It probably wasn't anyone called Arthur, but it's fun to think it might have been.

South Cadbury lies just off the A303 a few kilometres west of Wincanton and provides a parking area just to the south of the village (BA22 7HA). From the entrance, turn left and walk along the road until you can join a footpath on the left shortly after passing the end of Crangs Lane.

Cross a field to a gate, then follow the waymarked path across the next field to climb a stile in a hedge. Turn left, keeping to the edge of the fields with the distinctive ridge of Parrock Hill – a line of trees on the crest – over to your right. Coming abreast of Whitcombe Farm, follow the blue waymarkers right, down through the farmyard and along the lane to a road junction. Turn left, and on the brow of the hill continue up the steps to reach a stile opposite a row of cottages.

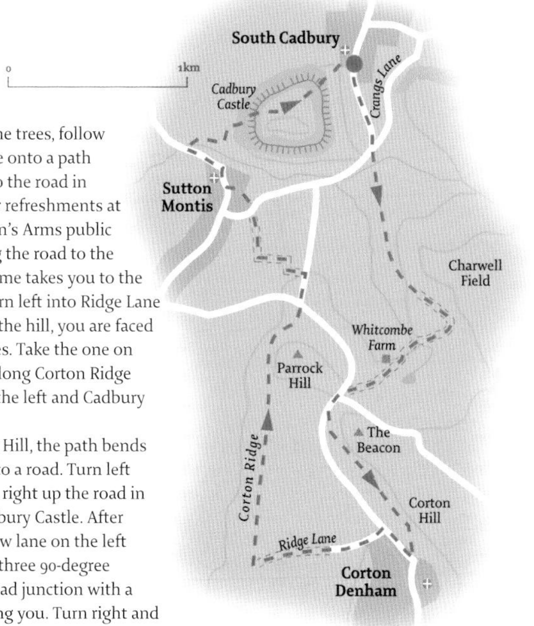

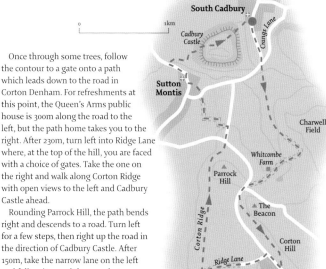

Once through some trees, follow the contour to a gate onto a path which leads down to the road in Corton Denham. For refreshments at this point, the Queen's Arms public house is 300m along the road to the left, but the path home takes you to the right. After 230m, turn left into Ridge Lane where, at the top of the hill, you are faced with a choice of gates. Take the one on the right and walk along Corton Ridge with open views to the left and Cadbury Castle ahead.

Rounding Parrock Hill, the path bends right and descends to a road. Turn left for a few steps, then right up the road in the direction of Cadbury Castle. After 150m, take the narrow lane on the left and follow it round three 90-degree corners to reach a road junction with a high stone wall facing you. Turn right and at the end of the wall go through the gate into an orchard.

Head straight out between the trees until you can turn left to a gate. Turn right on a road and walk past a church, bending left soon after, until you pass a house called Village End on your right. Some 60m beyond, a path sets off in the direction of the castle. Go right when you step into a field, then cross a stile to walk with a fence by your left hand, following it round the corner. After 100m, turn uphill to a gate into the woods. The path leads up the slope, through the defensive banking and on to the top.

There is evidence of at least 3000 years of occupation of the plateau and it's known that it was one of the last places in the southwest to fall to the Romans. Later, when the Romans had left, it became a fortress once again, with a 5m-thick defensive wall, gatehouse and large timber hall fit for a king. Whoever ruled from Cadbury Castle was certainly a man of stature – perhaps even Arthur himself.

Having soaked up the views, head for the opposite corner from the path by which you arrived and follow the track down towards the village. Turn right on the road to walk back to the start.

◂ Sutton Montis

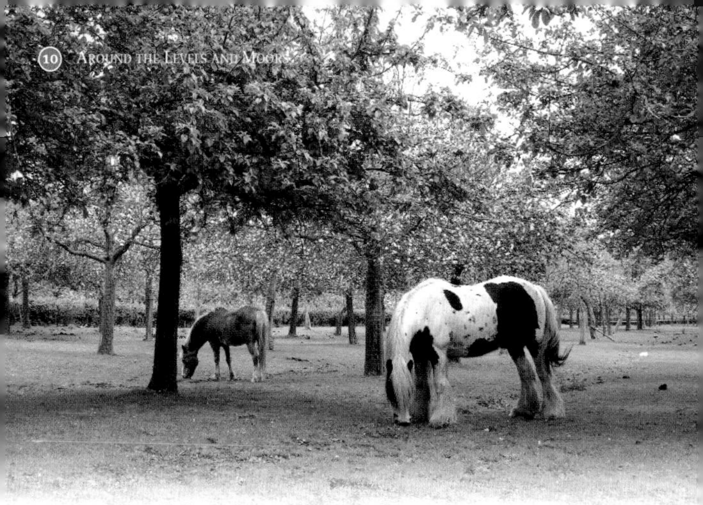

Stembridge's orchards

Distance **6km** Time **2 hours**
Terrain **fields, quiet country roads and stiles** Map **OS Explorer 129** Access **twice daily buses from Martock and Taunton**

Although the number of apple trees in Somerset has declined over the past century, you wouldn't think so when you walk around Stembridge. There are young orchards and mature orchards, and traditional 'standard' and modern 'bush' trees growing apples of all varieties. The village is also just a stone's throw from Burrow Hill Farm, where some of the county's best known cider (and cider brandy) is produced. The orchards are worth exploring at any time, but are particularly special during the spring blossom and autumn harvest.

Parking is at a premium in Stembridge, but you should find a spot across the road from the Rusty Axe pub (TA12 6BL). With the pub signpost behind you, walk down past the village noticeboard where, after 200m, a stile on the left leads into a field. Keep to the right-hand side, passing through two gates into an orchard, the first of many on this walk.

Climb a stile on the left when you come to it, and then head right to walk along an enclosed path with apple trees to your left. Go straight ahead on reaching a road, but only for a few steps to turn right onto a footpath, signed to Hawthorne Hill. The path leads through mature apple trees, then across three fields and another orchard to a road. Go right for 200m, then left onto a track beside a big farm building.

After passing through a gate, look for a path heading right after 50m along the side of the field before going through the gate at the far end. A hedged lane leads to a

◂ Orchard at Stembridge

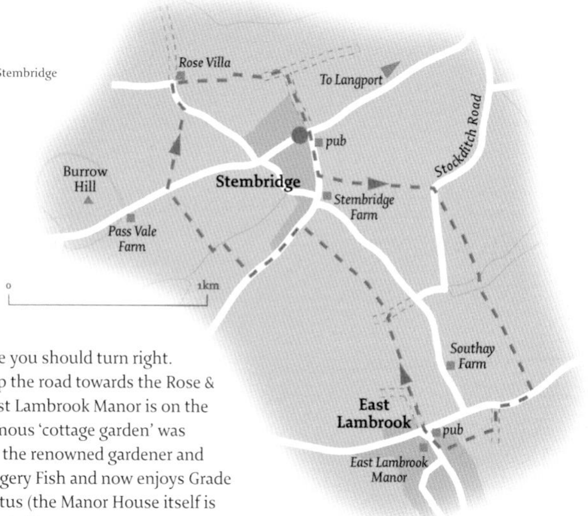

road where you should turn right. Walking up the road towards the Rose & Crown, East Lambrook Manor is on the left. Its famous 'cottage garden' was created by the renowned gardener and writer Margery Fish and now enjoys Grade I listed status (the Manor House itself is merely Grade II).

Fork left opposite the pub, cross a road and go up a track until it bends sharply left. Continue ahead up the side of a field to a gate in the hedge opening into an orchard. Keep to the left edge to reach a waymarked gate, where you turn right for a few steps, then left into a more mature orchard. Look for a stile in the hedge to your left, then turn left to walk up through the orchards, passing through gates along the way, until you find yourself walking on an enclosed path leading to a road.

Emerging by a brick shed with an old AA sign high on its gable – London is 133¾ miles from Stembridge apparently – turn left where, 250m past a school, a footpath sets off to the right. It leads up beside a young orchard with a good view of Burrow Hill, with its single tree on the top. On reaching the top of the field, go left into the corner, then turn right to reach a road.

The Somerset Cider Brandy Company is 350m to your left if you'd like to visit a traditional cider maker. Otherwise, cross into the field opposite and strike out in the direction of the red-roofed house on the far side, where a stile leads to a road. Go left for 140m to a fork and take a path which heads right in front of the gates to Rose Villa. Cross the first field to a stile, then aim for the far left corner of the next to join an enclosed path.

Turn right along the field edge to join a track between hedges. After 100m, turn right to walk down the lane back to the Rusty Axe.

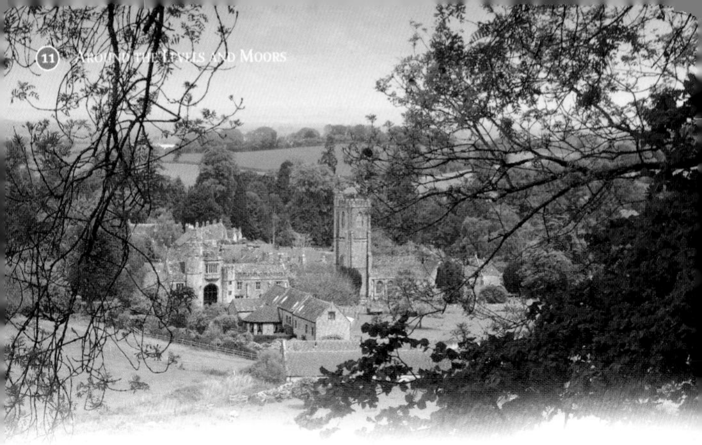

Ham Hill and Montacute

Distance **7km** Time **2 hours 30**
Terrain **fields and paths** Map **OS Explorer 129** Access **buses from Yeovil and South Petherton to Montacute where the walk can be joined midway**

The top of Ham Hill, once a prehistoric hillfort, is now a crazy maze of hollows and hummocks, created by centuries of quarry workings. In Victorian times there were around 200 family-operated quarries on the hilltop, but now just two remain. Stone from Ham Hill can be seen in buildings throughout the surrounding countryside, not least in Montacute which is almost entirely built of the honey-coloured 'hamstone'.

There are several free car parks along the top of Ham Hill and you should always be able to find a space (TA14 6RW). From the main entrance to the country park, where it is signed for the visitor centre and pub, take the left fork and immediately go through a gate on the left. A path leads to a war memorial, with stunning views, including Glastonbury Tor to the north and Alfred's Tower to the northeast.

Follow the broad path down from the memorial, turning right to pass the 'millennium stones', a modern-day stone circle, and on to the Prince of Wales pub. Beyond the front door, cross the road and head down the path signed Montacute. At the bottom of the steps, ignore a gate on the left and continue ahead to follow a path which undulates over the grassy knolls before merging with another path and bearing left to a clearing.

The two stone sculptures known as the Timestones are aligned so the rising sun on the longest day shines through the hole in the Celtic stone and onto the axehead. Continue through a gate onto grassland, bearing left by the information board, to follow the edge of three fields

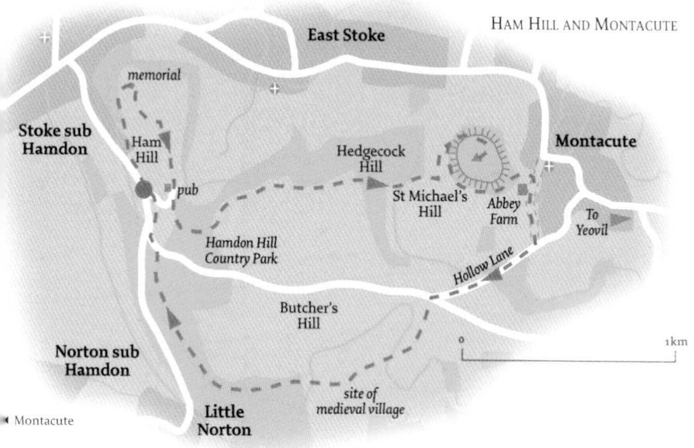

◂ Montacute

until the path heads through a gate into woodland and descends. Follow it all the way down to the bottom, going downhill whenever there is a choice, to cross a stile into a field.

To climb St Michael's Hill, bear left across the grass to a gate in the trees. From there a clear path leads round the hill to the top. The Romans called it Mons Acutus (meaning 'pointed hill') which is how the village got its name. The 'prospect' tower was built in the 18th century and an internal stairway allows you to climb to the top.

To descend the hill, you can take a path on the opposite side, but it's easier to return the way you arrived, turning left once back in the field to walk round the base of the hill to Abbey Farm. This was originally the gatehouse to Montacute Abbey which was razed during Henry VIII's Dissolution of the Monasteries. There is an easy detour into the village of Montacute by going left at this point, but our path heads right, along a gravel driveway, past Priory Pond and up a grassy track to Hollow Lane.

Go right for a few steps until a gate lets you into a field to walk beside the road. At the top, cross the road and head down the track between hedges to a gate into a field by an information board. In the valley ahead is the site of the 'lost' medieval village of Witcombe. Until the 16th century there were around 10 families living and farming here. All that remains today are the grassy outlines of houses and the silted-up village pond.

Head down past the pond, now behind a fence, and up the other side, leaving a gnarled marker post to your left. Turn right in the woods, then left by the stone marker depicting a Celtic warrior. The path now leads along the hillside for almost 1km to a car park. Turn left on the road for 100m, then take the path on the right through the grassy quarry workings, past a picnic area and back to the start.

Index